CINDERELLA TALES

AROUND THE WORLD

Global Understanding
Cultural Literacy

Cinderella Tales

AROUND THE WORLD

Global Understanding
Cultural Literacy

Ila Lane Gross

LEAPUSA.com
New York

This anthology would have been impossible to produce without the thoughtful efforts and continual help of Abby Adams.

Published in the United States of America
by Δ LEAPUSA.com
441 West End Avenue, 2G
New York, New York 10024
www.leapnyc.org

Fifth Printing 2012

Library of Congress Control Number: 2001135230
ISBN 0-9713649-1-5

Book design by Elizabeth Rosenberry

Printed and bound in China

This project was made possible by the generous support of The IBJ Foundation Inc. of the Industrial Bank of Japan, Limited.

Contents

6 China *Yeh-Shen*

12 Japan *Benizara and Kakezara*

20 Indonesia *Red Onion, White Onion*

31 India *The Black Cow*

39 Saudi Arabia *The Little Red Fish and the Clog of Gold*

46 Turkey *Keloglan*

59 Russia *Vasilisa the Beautiful*

69 Germany *Ashputtel*

78 South Africa *The Magic Horns*

86 South Africa *Bawa Merah*

92 Mexico *Domitila*

101 Brazil *Gata Borralheira*

109 Brazil *The Maiden and the Fish*

115 Chile *Maria Cinderella*

132 Bibliography

Yeh-Shen

China

YEH-SHEN

Once upon a time, there lived an old Chief named Wu who had two wives. After both wives gave birth to baby daughters, one of the wives became ill and died. Sadly, Chief Wu also died very soon after. Yeh-Shen, the orphan girl, was a beautiful, bright child with skin like ivory and eyes like dark pools of water. She was raised by her stepmother, who hated Yeh-Shen for being so beautiful and good. Her own daughter was very ugly and clumsy. To punish Yeh-Shen, the stepmother gave her all the hardest chores.

Yeh-Shen's only friend was a fish with golden eyes. Although the stepmother gave Yeh-Shen only scraps to eat, Yeh-Shen always saved some for her fish. One day, the stepmother discovered this secret and thought of a plan to catch Yeh-Shen's fish. She told Yeh-Shen, "Go collect some firewood, but leave your dirty coat here so the neighbors will not think we are poor." After Yeh-Shen left, the crafty stepmother slipped on the coat and hurried to the pond. The fish thought Yeh-Shen had come to feed him, so he jumped onto shore. But the stepmother stabbed the fish with a dagger and cooked it for dinner.

When Yeh-Shen saw that her fish had disappeared from the pond, tears spilled from her eyes and rolled into the water. Suddenly, a very old man appeared before her, saying, "Do not be sad that your fish is gone, for your pet has magical powers. Just kneel before your fish's bones, and you will receive whatever your heart desires." Before Yeh-Shen could ask him any questions, the old man rose up into the sky. Yeh-Shen went home to collect the bones of her friend, her throat choked with sadness.

Over the years, Yeh-Shen would often seek help from the fish's bones. When she was hungry, she would ask the bones for rice, and this is how she stayed alive.

One day, Yeh-Shen's stepmother gave her twice as many chores because it was time for the spring festival. As Yeh-Shen sewed and scrubbed, she dreamed of going to the festival and meeting the man she would marry. But her stepmother refused to let her go. She wanted her daughter to find a husband, and she knew that all the men would fall in love with the dark-eyed Yeh-Shen.

When the holiday arrived, the stepmother and daughter dressed in their finest silk and left for the banquet. Yeh-Shen knelt before the bones, and whispered, "Dear friend, I want to go to the festival, but I cannot wear these rags. How can I find clothing to wear to a feast?" Suddenly, she found she was dressed in a gown of the deepest blue, with a cloak of soft feathers draped over her slim shoulders. She looked down, and saw shimmering gold slippers on her tiny feet. As she flew out the door, the spirit of the bones reminded her, "Do not lose your golden shoes."

When she arrived at the festival, everyone stared in wonder, asking, "Who could this beautiful girl be?" Yeh-

Shen's stepsister said, "Mother, that looks like our Yeh-Shen!" Yeh-Shen ran away as fast as she could, hoping that they would not recognize her. As she flew down the path, one of the golden shoes slipped from her tiny foot. Her beautiful gown and cloak turned back to rags as she raced home, but she kept one golden slipper. When she arrived home, she found that the bones were silent. Yeh-Shen began to cry because she had lost her only friend.

In the meantime, a greedy villager had found the golden shoe and sold it to a merchant. The merchant then gave it to the king of T'o Han as a gift. The king was amazed at the shoe's beauty, and decided to find the woman who had lost this tiny slipper. He put the shoe back where it was found, and hid in the bushes with his attendants to see who would claim it. Every woman in the land tried to put on the shoe. However, no foot was small enough to fit in the delicate slipper. Finally, as the moon hid behind the clouds, Yeh-Shen appeared from the shadows and sank to her knees in front of the shoe. When the king saw the girl in rags, he was ready to throw her in prison as a thief. But when he glimpsed her sweet face and her tiny feet as she fled with the slipper, he quietly ordered his men to follow her.

Later that night, Yeh-Shen was shocked to find the king at her door. As she trembled with fear, the king asked in a gentle voice if she would try on the golden slipper. When Yeh-Shen slipped the shoe onto her little foot, her tattered clothes were again changed to a cloak of delicate feathers and a blue silk gown. The king looked into Yeh-Shen's dark eyes and fell madly in love with her. Soon after, the two were married.

However, fate was not as kind to Yeh-Shen's stepmother and stepsister. It has been said that they were crushed to death by a shower of stones.

Benizara and Kakezara

Japan

Benizara and Kakezara

A long time ago, there lived two sisters and a stepmother. One sister was named Benizara ("Crimson Dish"), and the other was named Kakezara ("Broken Dish"). Kakezara was the stepmother's own daughter, while Benizara was the daughter of a former wife. Benizara was gentle, kind, and honest, but her stepmother repaid this kindness with cruelty.

One day, the stepmother sent the two girls out to gather chestnuts. She handed a bag to Benizara and a bag to Kakezara. She did not mention that Benizara's bag had a big hole in the bottom. "Do not come back until you have filled your bags," she said sternly.

The girls headed for the mountains, picking up chestnuts as they walked. After a while, Kakezara's bag was filled with brown chestnuts, and she skipped home. Benizara was left alone. The honest Benizara picked up more and more chestnuts, but her bag was never full. She worked dutifully as the skies darkened. Night fell so quickly that she could barely see her quick little hands. Suddenly, she heard a rustling sound, *gasa gasa*, as if a wild animal were in the bushes. When she looked around in fear, she realized that she had gotten lost in the darkness. Benizara knew that crying would do her no good, so she started walking, hoping that she would find a house. Soon she saw a little light ahead of her. She followed the light, and came to a tiny house where an old woman sat spinning thread. Benizara explained her situation, and politely asked if she could stay the night there.

The old woman replied, "I would love to have you stay, but my sons are *oni*. They should be home any minute, and will surely eat you. I will help you find your way home instead." The old woman pointed out which road to take, and gave her directions home. Then she filled Benizara's bag with chestnuts, and handed her a little box and a bit of rice. "These chestnuts are for your mother. This little box is a magic box. If you ever need anything, say your wish aloud and tap the box three times. This rice is to protect you from my *oni* sons. If you meet them on your way home, chew up some rice and dribble it out of your mouth. Then you must lie on the ground and pretend to be dead."

Benizara thanked the kind old woman and headed home. After a while, she heard the distant sound of a flute coming toward her. She quickly chewed some rice and spread it around her mouth, doing as the old woman had told her. Then she lay down and pretended to be dead. Soon, a red *oni* and a blue *oni* came lumbering down the road. The red *oni* smiled gleefully, and said, "Brother! I smell a human!" and peered down at Benizara. "Ah, she's already rotten," he said sadly. "See, her mouth is filled with worms." And they continued down the road, piping on their flutes.

After they had disappeared, Benizara jumped up and kept walking until the sun came up. At home, the stepmother was happily thinking that wolves must have eaten Benizara. However, just as she was thinking these nasty thoughts, Benizara arrived home. The stepmother could not even scold her, because she was carrying a whole bag of chestnuts.

Some weeks later, a play was to be performed in their village. The stepmother decided to bring Kakezara to see the show, and left Benizara behind to do hundreds of chores. Benizara worked as hard as she could, trying to finish her washing, cooking, and cleaning before her step-mother returned. While she was working, some of her friends stopped by and asked if she would join them to see the play. Benizara sadly explained that she could not go because she had so many chores. Her friends said, "Don't worry, we'll all chip in and help you finish your work. Then you can go!" And so they finished a whole day's chores by working together.

As they were about to leave, Benizara noticed that her friends were all wearing beautiful kimonos. She looked down at her own rags and felt terribly embarrassed. She suddenly remembered the little box that the old woman had given her. When she tapped the box and asked for a kimono, a bright, beautiful kimono suddenly appeared. She slipped it on, and went to see the play. When she got there, she noticed Kakezara in the crowd, begging her mother for some sweet candies. Benizara threw her some, and Kakezara gobbled them up, not recognizing her own sister. A nobleman who had come to see the performance saw what had happened, and was intrigued by the beautiful girl.

The next day, the nobleman's grand procession came to the village, and stopped in front of Benizara's and Kakezara's house. The stepmother was thrilled, and dressed Kakezara in her finest silk kimono. When he came to their door and saw Kakezara, he said, "There should be two girls in this house. Please bring out the other one." The stepmother frowned, as she had hidden Benizara in the bathtub. However, she had to obey his command, so the stepmother pulled her out of the bathtub and set her in front of the nobleman. Benizara looked very poor and untidy next to the well-dressed Kakezara. The lord asked, "Which one of these girls attended the performance yesterday?" The stepmother cried "It was this one here, Kakezara!"

"No," said the nobleman, "it was not that one." But the stepmother insisted that it was. Very perplexed, he finally asked each girl to compose a poem. The nobleman placed a plate on a tray, and poured salt onto the plate. Then he stuck a pine needle in the pile of salt. "This is the subject for your poems. Let us hear your compositions," he declared.

Kakezara stepped forward, and in a loud voice sang:

Place a plate on that tray
Place some salt on that plate
Jab a pine needle in that salt
It will surely fall over.

Then she bopped the lord on the head and scurried away.

Next Benizara stepped forward, and in a soft, melodious voice sang:

A plate and a tray – oh!
A mountain rises up from the plate
On the plate, soft snow has fallen
And rooted in the snow drift,
Stands a lonely pine tree.

The nobleman was very pleased with this song, as it observed all the rules for poetic meter and was quite beautiful. He was so charmed by Benizara that he escorted her to his carriage, and they rode off to the nobleman's palace.

Kakezara's mother fumed in silence, watching the procession disappear. She threw Kakezara in a huge basket, saying, "Now you too may go to the lord's palace!" She set out on the road to the palace, dragging the basket so violently that Kakezara tumbled out and fell to her death in a ditch.

Red Onion, White Onion

Indonesia

RED ONION, WHITE ONION

Once upon a time, there lived a man and a woman and their daughter, Red Onion. While the girl was still small, the wife became ill and died. Her father soon remarried. His new wife had a daughter, White Onion (garlic in Indonesia) of about the same age as Red Onion. White Onion was very lazy, but very clever. She always figured out a way to get out of doing any work in the house.

One day the stepmother called the two girls to her, and said, " I must go to the market and sell our cabbages. While I am gone, go to the field and pick the rice, husk it, grind it, and make rice cakes for dinner."

After she had gone, White Onion sat down heavily on a bench, and said, "Dear, sweet sister, my head aches and standing in the sun is very hard. Please go pick the rice, and I will husk it after you are done, because I can sit in the shade of a palm tree and work."

Red Onion, seeing her stepsister in distress, said, "Of course I will help you. I will pick the rice." Going out into the hot field, Red Onion picked the rice kernel by kernel and, placing it in a basket, brought it home.

When she got home, her sister was sitting under the palm tree fanning herself. "Oh, dear sister," said White Onion, "I am so glad you have returned. I must go to grandmother's house to help her. While I am gone, please husk the rice or it will never be ready to cook in time for dinner."

"Of course I will help you," said Red Onion, "Go help Grandma."

White Onion sped away to the river and bathed herself in the cool water.

Meanwhile, poor Red Onion grew hot and sticky husking the rice. As she tossed the rice in the air to rid it of dust and leaves and broken stems, the rice was blown back into her face. Just as she finished, White Onion appeared all washed and fresh from the river. "Now we must grind the rice into flour. I would help but my back hurts from helping Grandma lift many bags and from cleaning her house."

"Don't worry," said Red Onion. "I will grind the rice and

you can build the fire in the oven. I have already cut wood for the fire."

The sweat dripped down Red Onion's back as she rolled the grinding stone back and forth over the grains of rice turning them into flour. White Onion looked up and saw her mother coming back from the market. "Quick, Red Onion, go to the river and clean yourself, I will finish before mother comes home. You have worked very hard."

"How kind you are White Onion. I will be no time at all. I will be back soon to help you take the rice cakes out of the oven, for it is very hot work," and off raced Red Onion to the river to wash.

White Onion quickly covered her arms in rice flour and messed her hair and dripped water on her head to look like sweat. Just as she was done, her mother came into the house. "Oh mother, I am glad you have returned. I have worked hard since you were gone while Red Onion has spent the day resting by the river in the shade of a large tree. I'm sure she will return soon to help me take the rice cakes out of the oven, as that is very simple work."

"My poor daughter, you work so hard and Red Onion is so lazy. I will beat her when she returns. She must learn a lesson."

Just as White Onion's mother was finishing saying this, Red Onion appeared from the river, freshly washed. The mother took one look at Red Onion all clean and fresh and her daughter all covered with flour and sweat. "How dare you disobey me, making your sister do all the work and you washing yourself and resting by the river all day?" Before Red Onion could say a word, the stepmother picked up a large stick and began to beat Red Onion on her back until she was covered with blood and could hardly stand. "Here are the dirty clothes," shouted the stepmother in a rage. "Take them to the river and wash them. When you are finished, come back and clean out the barn of all the dirt dropped by the animals."

Red Onion hobbled off crying, carrying the bundle of clothes with her. When she got to the river, she soaked herself in the cool water till the blood stopped running from her wounds. Then she washed her clothes as well as the bundle of dirty clothes her mother had thrust into her arms. She pounded each piece against a rock until it was clean and then spread them on the grass to dry. She was so tired from all the work that she soon fell asleep.

When she awoke, it was dark and she was frightened. She could not see and did not know which way to go. Stumbling along in the dark, she wandered for hours, getting more and more lost in the jungle, slipping on the muddy leaves that covered the floor of the jungle, and catching herself on hanging vines. Up and down through the trees she wandered. No light entered the jungle at night. The canopy of leaves hid the stars and moon. Strange birds called in the dark. She could feel the eyes of wild animals following her. She became more and more frightened.

Then, in the distance, she saw a dim light. Following it, she came to a clearing and a strange little house. All kinds of wild forest animals filled the clearing around the house. In the house was a little old woman. Looking out the door, she said, "Come in, my dear. Don't be afraid of the animals. They will not harm you. Come, you look very hungry. Would you like something to eat?"

"Oh, yes," replied Red Onion, walking by the animals with a little fear.

"Here is some nice, warm curried vegetables for you and some rice. Eat and rest. We will not harm you," said the old woman. First, Red Onion made a small offering to the gods, and then she sat down to eat.

Red Onion ate eagerly, as she had not eaten for many hours. Then she lay down on a mat to sleep. In the morning when she awoke, she found the old woman and all of the wild animals and birds gone. Rising, she cleaned the house, fetched firewood for the fire and water from the well, and then she went out into the old woman's garden and weeded the vegetables. In the evening, the old woman and the animals and birds returned. The old woman was pleased to find the house clean, the garden weeded, the fire in the hearth lit, ready to cook dinner, and fresh water in the water jar.

"How good you are," said the old woman. "Here, let us sit down and eat, for we have both had a long day." So saying, she took some food from the cupboard and heated it in a pot hung over the fire. Then they both sat down and ate dinner. After dinner, Red Onion felt very tired, but she insisted on washing the dishes before going to sleep.

For several weeks, Red Onion lived with the little old woman, helping her as best she could. As time passed, she missed her stepsister, White Onion, and her grandmother more and more. "I must go home to my grandmother; she is very old and may need my help," said Red Onion to the old woman. "You have been very kind, but I must go back. Can you help me find my way?"

"Of course I will help you," said the little old woman. "Come," she said to a little golden bird sitting on the window. "Show Red Onion the way home to her grandmother's house."

Then, turning to Red Onion, she handed her a pot, and said, "This is for you for all your help. Don't open it until you get home."

Following the beautiful golden bird, and carefully carrying the pot, Red Onion walked through the jungle. It no longer seemed frightening to her. Soon, in the distance, she saw her village and her grandmother in her small garden. When she looked round to thank the golden bird, it was gone.

Red Onion rushed up to her grandmother and kissed her. "How I have missed you, and what an adventure I have had. Come, sit down, Grandmother, and I will tell you all that has passed," and, so saying, she told the entire story.

"My good child," said the grandmother. "How I have missed you. I am so very happy that you are well. Now, come let us see what is in the pot."

Opening the pot, they both looked in it. The pot was full of gold and jewels and rings, and as they took out a piece to examine it, another that was even more beautiful quickly replaced it. "Now you are truly rich, my child, and will never have to work again," said the grandmother to Red Onion.

"Oh, but dear Grandmother, I am happy to work and help you, for you are very old," replied Red Onion.

"Come, my dear Red Onion, let me put some of these beautiful rings and earrings on you, as they are yours. My, how beautiful you look," sighed the old grandmother.

Just then White Onion arrived, looking very tired. Since Red Onion had disappeared, she had had to do all the work in the house and, being lazy, had done it badly. Her mother had begun to beat her just as she had beaten Red Onion. White Onion was miserable. When she saw her sister had returned, she was very happy. Now she wouldn't have to work so hard. Then she noticed all the jewels that she wore and became very jealous. "Well, sister, I see you have not been wasting your time since you left me to do all the work at home," whined White Onion.

"Oh, dear sister, you are wrong. Let me tell you what happened to me." And so saying, she told her sister the entire story.

"I, too, must go into the forest and find this old lady so that she can give me jewels and gold to decorate myself," said White Onion. Then, without another word, she rushed off into the jungle.

The branches of the jungle plants grabbed at her clothing. The vines grew long thorns that cut her skin, but White Onion would not be stopped. She wanted her own pot of jewels, and jealousy drove her on into the jungle. It grew dark, and still she rushed on, pushing the plants aside, kicking at the trees in her way, tearing the vines that tried to stop her. Then, in the distance, she, too, saw a dim light. Rushing forward, she saw the little house in the clearing. The clearing was filled with wild animals that snarled at her, but she rushed up to the house and pounded on the door. The little old woman opened the door and asked her to come in.

"I am very tired and hungry," said White Onion. "Bring me some food." Taking a dish from the hands of the old woman, she began to eat. When she was done she took a mat and fell asleep.

In the morning when White Onion awoke, the old woman and the animals were gone. White Onion went to the well and washed herself, then, going into the garden, she picked some vegetables and ate them. Being still tired she sat in the shade and fell asleep.

In the evening the old woman returned. She found nothing done. The garden unweeded, the dishes dirty, the water jar empty and no fire ready to cook dinner. White Onion stretched, and asked, "What is for dinner?"

The old woman fetched the wood and the water. She built the fire, cooked the meal, and then White Onion came into the house and helped herself to some food. After eating, she lay down on a mat and was soon asleep.

In the morning the old woman was still there when she

awoke. Yawning, White Onion said, "I really must go home. Can you give me a pot like you gave my sister and show me the way home?"

The old woman gave her a pot, warning her not to open it until she got home and then, calling a black crow, she told it to lead White Onion through the jungle to the village.

The crow flew ahead quickly, and White Onion stumbled on behind, trying not to get lost. Soon her curiosity got the better of her and she opened the jar. Out of it came frogs and toads and snakes. Dropping it, she ran on. The crow scratched at her and beat her with its wings. Scared and shaken, White Onion finally found her way back to the village. Falling into the arms of Red Onion, she cried and cried. "I will never be jealous of you again. I will share all of the work equally, for I now realize how lucky I am to have you as a sister."

Red Onion hugged White Onion and gave her earrings and rings so that she too would be beautiful. From that day forward they shared all the work and lived happily together.

The Black Cow

India

The Black Cow

Once upon a time, a Brahmin lived in a village in the foothills of the Himalayan Mountains. He had a lovely wife and a young son, named Vishnu. One day his wife became very ill and died. For a year, the Brahmin and his son lived alone. After a year, the Brahmin felt the period of mourning was sufficient, so he decided to get remarried. He found a woman of his caste who had a young daughter of about the same age as his son. He decided to marry the woman. The stepmother was very unkind to Vishnu.

Every day, the two children were sent out with the cattle to the forest so that they could find food to eat. In the evening, the children would return home hungry. The stepmother would feed her daughter and the Brahmin fine cakes filled with sweet meats and vegetables. But she would feed her stepson cakes made of mud with a little flour on top, so that the Brahmin would not know what she was doing. Vishnu would not complain, for he was very afraid of her and did not know what she would do to him if he spoke up to his father. Every day he grew hungrier and hungrier. As he walked in the forest with the cattle, he would cry and cry.

One of the cows, a fine black cow, noticed that he was crying, and asked, "Why do you cry every day? What is wrong?" At first Vishnu was very surprised that the cow could speak, but then he told her how hungry he was and what the stepmother was doing.

"Cry no more," she said, as she began to beat her hooves on the ground. Fine sweets of all kinds appeared, and Vishnu began to eat them greedily.

He picked up a handful and gave them to his stepsister saying, "Here, eat these, for they are very good. Only you must not tell your mother about the cow, as she might become very angry." The young girl promised to keep it a secret.

Soon the stepmother noticed that, instead of getting thinner and thinner, Vishnu was growing tall and strong and healthy. She immediately suspected that he was drinking the cow's milk. This made her very angry, and she decided to spy on him. So she called her young daughter to her, and said, "Watch your brother carefully. I am sure he is drinking the cow's milk when you go to the forest every day."

The young girl did not know what to do. She was obliged to obey her mother, but she had promised her stepbrother not to tell about the black cow and the sweets. In the end, she told her mother about the cow, as it was worse to disobey her mother than to break a promise to her brother.

When the Brahmin came home that evening, the stepmother asked him to sell the black cow. The Brahmin agreed. Vishnu was very upset and went to the barn to say goodbye to the cow. Crying, he threw his arms around her neck and sobbed. "Why are you crying now?" asked the cow.

"My stepmother knows how you have helped me and has talked my father into selling you tomorrow," Vishnu.

"Get up on my back," said the cow. "Hold tight while I take you deep into the forest where you will be safe and I can take care of you."

Vishnu climbed on her back, and they rode off into the night. Deep in the forest, they stopped at a clearing. A brook with sweet water ran through it, and soft, green grass covered the ground. There they stayed, safe and secure, for many weeks.

Near the clearing in the forest was a deep hole in the ground. In this hole lived the Great Snake, who, along with a bull, holds up the entire universe. Every day, the black cow poured her sweet milk into this hole for the Great Snake to drink.

The Great Snake was very pleased with the milk, and said to himself, "I wonder, who is giving me this sweet milk? I think I will go up to the earth to see who it is." The Great Snake stuck his head out of the hole and looked around. He saw a young boy standing beside a grazing black cow. "Is it you who gives me the delicious milk every day?" asked the snake in a soft voice. The cow nodded her head.

"What can I give you in return for the sweet milk you gave to me unbidden?" asked the snake.

"Nothing for me," said the cow, "but could you dress my son," nodding toward Vishnu, "in a suit of gold? Also, could you make his body shine as if it, too, were gold?"

"This wish I can easily grant," said the Great Snake. In an instant, the boy was dressed in gold, from the cloth on his head to the shoes on his feet. The snake then uncoiled himself and glided back into his hole in the ground.

The cow soon thought better of her wish. Both she and Vishnu now feared that robbers might harm them. They looked cautiously over their shoulders and started at any strange or unexpected sound.

One day, as Vishnu was combing his long, golden locks after bathing in the river, some of his hair fell into the water. The strands were so bright and shining that a fish swallowed them. A fisherman further down the river caught the fish. He took it, with many others, to sell at the king's palace. The palace servants bought the fish and took it to the kitchen. There, it was cut open and the golden hairs fell out. Everyone was amazed.

The princess heard about the golden hairs and came to see them. "Oh, how beautiful they are," she sighed. "I would love to see the owner of such beautiful hair." She sighed again, and said, "Now I will never be happy again." She sadly walked away.

The servants noticed how sad the princess had become. They quickly rushed off to find the fisherman. "Fisherman, fisherman," they all shouted at once. "Where did you catch your fish today?"

The fisherman pointed up the river, and said, "Up and down the river, in that direction."

Soon fisherman and local people were all sent out in every direction by Queen Bundo Kandung to see what they could find. They looked up the river and down the river. Then, far in the distance, one man saw a shining object in the shallow part of the river. He slowly rowed closer and closer. Soon, he could see it was a shining boy. He called out to the boy, "Come closer, so that I might see you clearly." The boy either did not hear him or just ignored him. The man rowed his boat closer, and said again, "Come closer, so that I might see you clearly." This time the boy looked at the man, but did not move. The man rowed even closer to the boy and said yet again, "Come closer so that I might see you clearly." At this, Vishnu waded out to the boat. The man leaned forward and grabbed Vishnu, tied him up with cord, and pulled him into the boat. The man rowed back down the river to the palace.

When Vishnu arrived at the palace, the princess rushed out to see him. As soon as he saw the beautiful princess, he fell in love and could think of nothing but her. She, on seeing him, also fell deeply in love. The young couple was married. They lived for several weeks in great happiness, thinking of nothing but each other.

One day, someone in the palace offered them sweets made from milk curd just like the ones the black cow had given Vishnu in the forest. He suddenly remembered his old friend, the black cow who had taken such good care of him. Very upset that he had not thought of her for days, Vishnu rushed from the palace and ran into the forest to look for her. Finally, he arrived at the clearing. In the clearing was only a pile of cow bones.

Vishnu threw himself down on the ground in despair. He then gathered all the bones together into a funeral pyre. He sobbed, "I have deserted you, and now you are gone. I will burn your bones and throw myself on your burning pyre."

With these words, the old black cow came out of the forest. "Stop," she said. "I only put those old bones there to see if you really cared for me. Now I see you really care." The princess and the king and all the servants who had been following behind arrived just at this moment. They praised the cow, and then all sat down for a feast. At the end of the feast, the cow went one way, and Vishnu and his princess returned to the palace with the king to live happily.

The Little Red Fish and the Clog of Gold

Saudi Arabia

The Little Red Fish and the Clog of Gold

Once upon a time, a fisherman lived near a great river. His wife had died some time ago, but not before she gave him a pretty little daughter. A widow and her daughter lived nearby, and they would often come over to comb the young girl's hair. The motherless girl persuaded her father to marry the widow, as she could not bear to see him wash his own clothes and cook his own food.

As soon as the wedding was over, the new wife began to hate the young girl. The girl had beautiful golden skin and quick hands, while her own daughter was sallow and clumsy. The stepmother fed the girl only crumbs and would not give her soap to wash herself. The girl never said one word of complaint. She would only close her eyes, patiently thinking, "I did this with my own hands, so I will save myself with my own mind."

One day, as she returned from the river with a basket of fish, a little red fish peeked out and said,

> "Throw me back into the water
> And you will always be my daughter."

The girl was filled with wonder and fear, and threw the fish back into the river. She thought to herself, "A good deed is always seen by Allah." The fish emerged from the water, saying,

> "I am your new mother, so when you are sad
> Come to the river, and I will make you glad."

When the girl gave the basket of fish to her father, he asked why one fish was missing. The young girl said, "Father, the red fish dropped from my basket." Her father forgave her, but her stepmother said that if she did not return with the fish she would place a curse on her. The girl walked to the river, her eyes filled with tears.

When she called out for the little red fish, she appeared and said, "You will be rewarded for your patience. Take this gold piece and give it to your stepmother. She will not harm you." The girl gave the gold to her stepmother, so she was not punished.

Some years later, the rich master of the merchant's guild announced that his daughter was to be married. Every girl wanted to go to the bride's party. This was where mothers brought their unwed daughters to be seen by the mothers of unwed sons. The fisherman's wife scrubbed her daughter's face and dressed her in a fine gown, hoping she would find her own daughter a husband. As soon as they left for the party, the girl hurried down to the river to ask her fish for help.

The red fish gave her a small bundle, saying, "Here is everything you need. But remember: your stepmother must not see you." When she opened the bundle, out fell a beautiful gown of green silk with threads and sequins of gold. She also found a comb of pearl for her hair and golden clogs for her feet. She quickly washed and dressed herself, then rushed to the feast.

Every woman at the party wondered who the graceful beauty could be. They decided that she must be the governor's daughter. Giving her sweet almonds and honey-cakes, they placed her in the seat of honor. The stepmother and her daughter stood in the corner with the wives of peasants, weavers and peddlers.

The stepmother thought, "Allah be praised, that girl looks like my husband's daughter!" But before she could be sure, the girl fled the party. As she raced home over the bridge, one of the golden clogs fell from her foot into the river. There was no time to waste, so she continued on her way.

The golden clog rolled and tumbled in the river's current until it came to rest in a pool near the king's palace. The next day, the prince took his stallion to drink at the pool and found the shining clog. He dreamed of the beautiful girl who owned such a precious little shoe. Holding the clog close to his beating heart, he returned to the palace. The prince said to his mother, "I want to marry the girl who owns this golden clog."

The queen replied, "My son, you shall have her."

Every day, the prince's mother searched for the girl with the golden clog. She went to every house, measuring every girl's foot against the little shoe. She traveled from the houses of nobles, merchants and goldsmiths to the huts of craftsmen, weavers and fishermen. When the stepmother heard that the queen was coming, she bathed her

daughter, dressed her, and rimmed her eyes with kohl. She dragged the fisherman's daughter into the bakehouse in the ground, hissing, "Don't you dare move!"
When the queen arrived, she measured the daughter's foot. Suddenly, a rooster ran into the yard, crowing,

> "Ki-ki-ki-ko!
> Let the queen know
> That the beauty's hid below!"

The queen sent her servants to search for the girl. They found her in the bakehouse, her beautiful face glowing through the piles of ash. The servants brought her to the queen, and they slipped the golden clog onto her foot. The queen smiled, saying, "This beauty is now betrothed to my son."

Anger boiled in the stepmother's stomach. She flew to the bazaar in a rage and bought a vial of medicine that would make someone's hair dissolve, their skin smell like death, and their insides fall from their body. When the stepmother prepared the girl for her wedding, she forced this medicine down the girl's throat. After a joyful wedding procession, with music, singing and clapping, the bride arrived at the palace. When the prince lifted her veil, her beauty shone like a full moon. Her hair was like a cloth of gold threads, and her skin smelled of amber and roses. She lifted the hem of her gown, and gold pieces spilled from her body. The stepmother was furious that her plan did not work.

The master merchant's son heard of this beautiful girl, and decided he wanted her sister for his bride. The stepmother thought, "If the medicine made my stepdaughter's hair into gold, why not do the same for my child?" She hurried back to the bazaar and bought twice as much medicine. On the day of the wedding, the merchant's son lifted her veil and a stench of death filled the room. Her hair came out in his hands, and he sent her away, covered in her filth.

As for the prince and the fisherman's daughter, they lived happily ever after, and were blessed with seven children.

KELOGLAN

Turkey

Keloglan

Once upon a time, a sultan had two wives. His first wife had one son. His second wife had two sons. One day, the first wife became very ill and soon died. The second wife thought about her two sons. She realized that if she wanted them to prosper, she would have to get rid of the son of the first wife.

The son of the first wife was a fine young man. He had but one passion, and that was horses. He had raised a colt from the stables of the *Djinn*. The horse rode faster than the wind, some said even faster than a flash of lightening across the sky. One day, after riding his young horse, the prince returned it to the stables. As he looked at it, he noticed that it was shedding tears.

"Why are you crying?" he asked the horse.

"Your stepmother is planning to poison you with a goose this evening," replied the horse.

"Do not worry," said the sultan's first son.

That evening, the queen prepared three fine geese. On

each, she poured a flavorful sauce; only, in one of the sauces, she added a deadly poison. All three sons sat down to eat, and the queen, smiling, served them. The first son looked at his goose and smelled its fine sauce. It looked the same as the others, but he felt it was best to be safe, rather than sorry. So the first son switched his goose with the goose of one of his half brothers when he was not looking. The half brother took one bite and fell down dead even before a groan could escape. Now the first son of the sultan knew that he should always listen to his young horse.

Horrified, the queen burst into tears of sorrow and rage. She went to the midwife who had helped her prepare the poison. "What shall I do? How can I get rid of the first son of the sultan? I hate him more than ever," she raged.

"Dig a great hole in the ground, just inside the front door. Cover the hole with a carpet so that no one can see it. When the first son falls into the hole, he will break his neck and die," advised the midwife.

That day, as with every day, the sultan's first son rode out on his beautiful *Djinn* horse, racing the wind from one end of the kingdom to the other. When he came home, he removed the saddle and looked up into the face of his horse. Again he noticed that the eyes of his horse were filled with tears, and that they ran down his muzzle. "Why do tears fall from your eyes?" he asked.

"The wicked queen is going to try to kill you again. She has dug a hole inside the front door and when you stride in, you will fall into the hole and break your neck," said the horse.

"Nothing will happen to me now that I know," said the prince, and he strode toward the palace. When he got to the front door, he jumped halfway into the room. Unfortunately, his half brother was just behind him and stepped onto the rug hiding the hole. Into the hole he plunged headfirst, breaking his neck. His mother was distraught and cried with rage and sorrow. She tore at her clothes and wailed, but nothing would bring him back to life.

After burying her second and last son, the sultan's wife's rage grew greater and greater. "If it wasn't for the first son's magic horse, none of this would have happened. I must get rid of that horse!"

The midwife and the doctor consulted with her and decided on a plan. The queen boiled barley chaff, the skins that coat the barley seeds. She then drained the chaff and threw it away. She reheated the water and bathed in it. Her skin became a sickly yellow. Next she put dry bread under her mattress and got into bed. The sultan came and looked at his wife. "You look so very ill," he said. "I hope you will not die, as did my first wife. Call the doctor."

The doctor came and rolled the queen around on the bed. The stale bread made cracking noises. "Oh, mighty Sultan," he said, "I fear your wife is very ill. You can hear that her ribs are broken. She needs the meat of a tender horse to cure her."

The sultan called his son to him, and said, "Your stepmother will die if she does not eat the meat of a young horse. We want to kill your horse to save the life of the queen."

"The life of the queen is worth more than my horse, and of course you may have him. But, may I ride him one last time before you kill him?" asked the prince.

"Of course," said the sultan. With that, the prince went off to the stable and saddled up his horse. He tightened up the girdle of the horse until the horse's stomach almost touched its back. Then, mounting the horse, he rode it up and down until it was all warmed up. Turning away from the palace, he said, "Open before me, oh path." Within an instant, the palace, the kingdom, and the entire lands were all far behind him.

Soon they arrived at the seashore, and the young man dismounted. "We must part," said the *Djinn* horse. "Before I leave, take seven hairs from my mane. When you need me, burn one of the hairs, and I will come." Then the horse galloped off down the beach, leaving the first son alone.

The young son did not want to be recognized, so he bought the stomach of a sheep from a butcher and stretched it over his head so that he would look bald. He then went in search of a job. He was soon hired as a watchman for a farmer who owned many orange orchards. He went by the name of Keloglan, or baldhead, since he did indeed appear to be bald. Every once in a while, he would miss his fine horse. Going where no one could see, he would burn one horse's hair. As the smoke rose, the horse would appear all saddled and bridled and ready to be mounted.

Then he would get on the horse and ride up and down the beach like the wind. The prince's heart would swell with happiness as he sped on his steed.

The king of this land had a beautiful castle by the sea, and every evening, his daughters would all go to the beach to bathe in the soft foaming water. One day, the king's youngest daughter spied Keloglan as he dashed by on his horse. The sight of him touched her heart, and she thought, "That is the man I wish to marry." Calling her sisters together, she asked, "Don't you all wish to marry? We must ask our father when he next comes to visit with us."

A few days later, the king came to visit his daughters. "Yaba," they said, "do you not remember the story that we were told as children, in which the woman who was free to have whatever she desired wanted most to marry. Won't you allow us to marry?"

The king smiled, and said, "Yes, I will allow you to marry." So saying, he sent messengers throughout the kingdom to announce that the princesses were going to choose their husbands, and every young man who was not married should appear at the palace the next day.

The next day, every unmarried youth appeared below the windows of the palace. As they paraded by, the princesses peeped out, and each selected the man she wished to marry. One chose the son of a pasha, another chose the son of a famous minister of the king, another decided on a tall handsome nobleman, but the youngest princess chose Keloglan, a mere gardener's boy who watched over orange fields. The next day there was a huge wedding, and all the princesses were married.

After the wedding, the king left and went home. He was very sad because his youngest and favorite daughter had chosen to marry a lowly gardener. He grieved and grieved until he made himself sick. Doctors and astrologers were called to the palace to see if they could cure the king. Finally, after much examination of the king and many conferences between everyone, the doctors announced that only the milk of the white gazelle could cure the king of his illness.

Now, it so happens that gazelles are quite rare, and that white gazelles are even three times more rare. The king's ministers called all the sons-in-law of the king together and told them that only the milk of the white gazelle would save the life of the king. The sons-in-law all rode out in search of a white gazelle. They rode to the left, and they rode to the right. Not a deer or a gazelle of any kind did they find. Meanwhile, Keloglan went into the forest and burned a magic hair from his horse, and instantly, the horse appeared. He told the horse about the king and asked him to find a white gazelle. No sooner had he spoken than an entire herd of white gazelles appeared like cotton in a field. The gazelles all lay down to rest in front of Keloglan.

Just at that moment, all the king's other sons-in-law rode up. "Can we have just one?" asked the sons-in-law.

"You can for a price," said Keloglan.

"Name your price," they said.

"I only want to brand each of you on your lower back with a very small brand," said Keloglan.

"That is a very strange request," they said. "But no one will see it, and so why not?" they all agreed.

Keloglan branded every son-in-law on the back, then gave each one a white gazelle to milk. The sons-in-law milked the gazelles and brought the milk to the king to drink. He took one sip of the milk and could drink no more.

"It is too bitter to drink," sighed the king. Meanwhile, Keloglan milked another gazelle and brought this milk in a bowl to the king. The king drank it all, saying it was sweet, and shortly thereafter, he was fully recovered.

All remained peaceful in the kingdom for many months following the recovery of the king. Then, one day, another misfortune befell the kingdom. A neighboring kingdom invaded the king's land. All the sons-in-law of the king mounted their horses and went to defend the kingdom. Only Keloglan was left behind.

"What about me?" he asked the sons-in-law. "Can you not give me a horse to ride and weapons with which to fight?"

So the sons-in-law gave him a lame horse, mounted him backward on the horse, then rode off to battle against the invading army.

Keloglan burned a magic hair, and instantly his *Djinn* horse appeared with weapons, armor, and a shield. Keloglan rode off into battle on his horse, defeating all around him. He was so glorious in his armor and so strong a warrior that no one could guess that he was Keloglan, the gardener's assistant. As he was fighting, he saw someone was about to kill the king, who was in the middle of the battle. Urging his horse, he arrived in time to slay the man who was about to kill the king. In so doing, he was slightly cut on his hand. The king wrapped the cut with his own handkerchief, and Keloglan continued to fight. In the end, Keloglan defeated the invading army.

When the battle was over, everyone rode back. Keloglan returned riding backward on the lame horse. The king, however, noticed that his hand was bandaged with his handkerchief. He then realized immediately it was Keloglan who had saved his life.

"Keloglan, sit next to me this evening at the victory feast," said the king. "Now, Keloglan, tell me your whole story. You are obviously not whom you seem to be." So Keloglan told him the whole story about how he was the son of the sultan and all about the events of his life leading up to his marriage to the princess.

Upon returning to his home to prepare for the feast, Keloglan removed the sheep's stomach from his head, bathed and dressed in the rich silken clothes of a prince. He strode out of the doorway of the youngest princess's house with the fine bearing and grace of a king. The other princesses were very upset and ran to their father. "The youngest princess has a lover," they all said. The king told the whole story of Keloglan. That quickly ended the chatter of the other princesses.

In the king's palace, there was a beautiful guest hall decorated with colorful tiles and paintings and gold and silver decorations. Mirrors covered half the walls and were set in the tiles. They all glittered with the light from a thousand candles. Seated in the great hall were all the ministers, *pashas*, princes, and judges dressed in fine silken robes embroidered with gold and silver threads. Each was seated according to his rank. In the middle of all this splendor sat the sons-in-law. No one thought that the tall, princely person who sat next to the king was Keloglan. Then the slaves, dressed in silken robes, brought in the food on golden trays. Odors of cumin, coriander, saffron, ginger, rosemary, thyme, and sweet fruits rose invitingly in the air from the golden platters of food. The king noticed that Keloglan did not eat any of the splendid dishes. "Why do you not eat, Keloglan?" asked the king.

All of the sons-in-law looked up with amazement when they heard the king address the noble man sitting next to him as Keloglan. Whispering into their beards, they all asked, "Can this be Keloglan?"

Again, the king asked, "Why do you not eat Keloglan?"

"As the son of a sultan, I cannot sit down and eat with my slaves," he said.

"What do you mean?" asked the king. "What slaves do you mean?"

"Why him and him and him," said Keloglan, pointing to all his brothers-in-law.

"How can this be?" asked the king. "Since when did you make them your slaves?"

"Since the day that I branded each of them on their lower back," he said. "Ask them each to raise their robes and you shall see. If I am not telling the truth, you may cut off my head."

The king checked the back of each of his sons-in-law, and it was true to the very last one. The king ordered them all out of the great hall in disgrace. They were required from that day forward to do just as Keloglan ordered. The king placed Keloglan upon the throne to rule in his place, as he was growing old.

How often it comes about that fortune turns a man's fate around!

Vasilisa the Beautiful

Russia

Vasilisa the Beautiful

Once upon a time in a village in Russia, there lived a merchant, his wife and their beautiful daughter Vasilisa. When Vasilisa was eight, her mother became very ill. Just before she died, she called Vasilisa to her, and said, "Take this doll. Hide it and keep it safe. It will look after you and help you, but you must never let anyone know about it." Vasilisa kissed her mother one last time before she died. Vasilisa and her father mourned the death.

Several months after Vasilisa's mother died, her father remarried. He married a widow with two daughters just a little older than Vasilisa. The stepmother and her stepsisters were very mean to Vasilisa and made her do lots of work. They hoped that making Vasilisa work in the fields would make her thin and wrinkled and tan from the sun, but each day Vasilisa grew more beautiful, while her stepsisters, who sat all day, grew more and more ugly.

Every day, Vasilisa went out into the fields with the doll. Vasilisa would sit under a tree in the shade or pick wild flowers while the doll would weed the garden, water the plants, haul the water and clean the house. Every day, Vasilisa would take her food and put it in her pocket. Then at night after everyone went to bed, Vasilisa would take the doll out and feed her the best bits of food. She would often go hungry in order to feed the doll. Sitting together, Vasilisa would tell the doll how unhappy she was, and the doll would give Vasilisa advice.

Years passed, and Vasilisa grew more and more beautiful. Many men in the village wanted to marry her, but her stepmother and her stepsisters were jealous. Her stepmother said, "You may not marry until my daughters, who are older, are married first." One day, Vasilisa's father had to go away on a long trip. When he was gone, the stepmother closed the house. She moved to a new house, away from the village at the edge of the forest.

In the forest lived the witch Baba Yaga in a little hut at the edge of a clearing. Baba Yaga ate people the way we eat chickens. The stepmother would often send Vasilisa into the forest to fetch wood or wild mushrooms. She hoped that Baba Yaga would catch Vasilisa and eat her, but every day Vasilisa would return home safe and sound. This was because the doll would advise her where to go to avoid the witch.

One night, the stepmother gave each girl a task to do. She told her eldest daughter to make lace, her second daughter to knit socks, and Vasilisa to spin a huge basket of wool. She scolded them saying, "You must all finish your tasks before you may go to bed or I will punish you in the morning." Then she quickly went to bed, leaving them with one small candle.

Soon the candle burned out, and they could not see to do their work. "Please," pleaded the eldest sister, "Go ask Baba Yaga for a candle, so that we can all finish our work."

"Go, go, or we will all be punished!" cried the second sister, pushing Vasilisa out of the room.

Vasilisa went to her room. Crying, she fed her doll the best bits of food she had hidden in her pocket. "They are sending me to Baba Yaga and I will die," wept Vasilisa. The doll's eyes glowed and lit the room.

"Don't be afraid," said the doll. "I will protect you."

Vasilisa walked through the woods, shaking with fear. Suddenly, a horseman galloped past. He was white-faced, dressed all in white and riding a white horse. Just as dawn came, a second horseman, red-faced, dressed in red and riding a red horse, galloped by faster than the first. Vasilisa continued to walk all day and all night and all the next day until she came to the hut of Baba Yaga just as evening was approaching. The fence around the hut was made of human bones, and the fence posts all had human skulls with staring eyes. The doorposts were human legs, the hinges were hands, and the lock a human mouth. The hut stood on giant chicken legs.

Vasilisa stood frozen with fear. Suddenly, a third horseman all in black on a black horse rode up to Baba Yaga's hut and disappeared. Night came, but it wasn't dark, as all the heads on the fence posts began to glow with an eerie light. Vasilisa stood frozen on the spot. A cold sweat dripped down her back.

A terrible rumble of noise came from the forest. The trees shook and cracked, and the grass bent from the force of the sound. Baba Yaga came flying out of the forest, riding a mortar and pestle, sweeping away her tracks with a broom. She sniffed the air and bellowed, "Fie, fie! I smell a Russian."

"Tis I," whispered Vasilisa with fear. "My stepsisters have sent me to borrow a candle."

"I know your sisters," hissed Baba Yaga with a laugh. "Vasilisa, I will give you a light, but first you must work for me. If you don't do all I ask, I will eat you." With a whistle, the gate opened, and Baba Yaga rode in with Vasilisa following behind. The gates locked behind her.

Baba Yaga went into the hut and sat down. "Feed me, Vasilisa, for I am very hungry." Vasilisa found the oven filled with meats and stews, which she served to Baba Yaga. She ate everything, leaving only a crust of bread and a little bit of cabbage soup for Vasilisa. "Tomorrow, I want you to clean the house and yard, cook me dinner and collect a bushel of wheat from the corn bin." Then Baba Yaga went to bed, leaving Vasilisa crying.

"Oh, dear doll, please help me," wept Vasilisa, as she fed all the food left for her to the doll.

"Don't cry," said the doll. "I will help you."

In the morning, Baba Yaga rode out into the forest, leaving Vasilisa with all the work to do. Looking about the hut, Vasilisa was surprised at all the food and beautiful things.

As she turned around, her doll was sweeping up the last of the chaff from the wheat and all the work was done. "All you must do is cook the dinner with mother's blessing, and all will be fine," said the doll.

"You have saved my life," said Vasilisa to her doll and hid her away gently in her pocket. In the evening, Vasilisa set the table and waited for the arrival of Baba Yaga. The man on the black horse rode up to the hut and disappeared and night fell. The heads on the fence began to give off their eerie glow. Baba Yaga arrived and, sitting down, called for her dinner. Vasilisa served her and showed her the bushel of wheat. Three pairs of hands appeared out of nowhere and carried the wheat away.

"Tomorrow, you must clean up all the dust someone threw into the wheat bins, or I will eat you," hissed Baba Yaga. Then, finishing her dinner, she went off to bed.

Vasilisa began to cry, "What will I do? I can never remove all the dust from the bins."

"Don't cry," said the doll, "I will help you with the task."

In the morning after Baba Yaga rode away, Vasilisa went to the bins, but the doll had already cleaned them for her. When Baba Yaga returned for supper that night, she was amazed at what Vasilisa had accomplished. "You may ask me any question you want and I will answer it."

"Who is the white horseman?" asked Vasilisa.

"He is dawn and my helper," replied Baba Yaga.

"Who is the red horseman?"

"He is the sun, and he is my helper."

"Who is the black horseman?"

"He is night, and he is my helper. Do you have any more questions?" Vasilisa wanted to know about the hands, but did not ask out of fear.

"Well," said Baba Yaga, "now that I have answered your questions, you must answer mine. How did you accomplish all the tasks I asked of you?"

"I did it with the help of my mother's blessing," replied Vasilisa.

"What!" screamed Baba Yaga, "I won't have any blessed ones in my house! Get out! Here, take this skull torch and be gone," shouted Baba Yaga.

Taking the skull torch and lighting it from the fence, Vasilisa and her doll began to walk home through the forest. Before the night was done, Vasilisa arrived back at the house where her stepmother and stepsisters were living. There was no light in the house. Vasilisa entered the house with the skull torch. The stepmother and stepsisters greeted her warmly, and said, "There has been no light or heat since you have gone." With that, the skull glowed even brighter and looked at the stepmother and stepsisters. Following them around the room, the eyes of the skull burned them all to ashes.

Terrified, Vasilisa fled back to the town, where a kind old lady asked her to come and live with her. Vasilisa lived with the old lady while she waited for her father to return. In the spring, Vasilisa asked the old lady for flax to weave into linen. She wanted to give the kind old lady a present. When Vasilisa was done, the linen was so fine that the old lady said, "This is too fine for me. I will take it as a gift to the czar, as it is too fine for me to use."

When she got to the palace, the czar saw her walking back and forth in front of the palace and asked her to come in side. "Here is some fine linen I wish to give to you," said the old lady humbly.

"This is wonderful linen. I would like it made into shirts for me," commanded the czar. The linen was cut up to be made into shirts, but no one wanted to sew the linen because it was too fine. The czar commanded that the old lady to return to the palace. "You wove the linen, and now you must sew it into shirts, as no one else will do it because it is so fine," explained the czar.

The old lady returned home and told Vasilisa what had happened. Vasilisa took the linen and went into her room, locking the door. She quickly sewed all the shirts for the czar. As soon as she had finished, the old lady took them to the czar. Vasilisa washed and dressed and combed her beautiful long hair and sat at the window, waiting for the old lady to return. Instead, a servant came and asked her to come meet the czar, as he wanted to thank her personally for the shirts.

When Vasilisa arrived at the palace, the czar took one look at her and fell in love. He asked her to marry him. She agreed. Shortly afterward, her father returned and, hearing all that had happened, rushed to his daughter. Vasilisa was so very glad to see her father that the czar asked him to come live with them in the palace.

Ashputtel

Germany

Ashputtel

Once there was a rich man who had a beautiful, kind wife. She suddenly became ill, and when she felt that the end was near, she called her only daughter to her bedside. She stroked her hair, and said, "Always be a good girl, and I will watch over you from heaven." Upon saying this, she closed her eyes and died. She was buried in the garden, and the little girl visited her grave every day, watering it with tears. Although she was very sad, she was still always good and kind to everything and everyone around her.

Months passed, and by springtime, her father had married a new wife. This wife had two daughters of her own whose faces were bright and fair, but whose hearts were dark and foul. They would laugh at her, squealing, "Get away from us, dirty kitchen maid!" They took away her fine clothes and gave her an old gray frock to wear. The poor little girl was forced to do hard work from sunrise to sunset, while her sisters mocked her. She would sew the clothes, bring the water, make the fire, cook the meals, and wash the dirty laundry. As she was made to sleep in the hearth among the ashes, she was always dirty, and her sisters called her Ashputtel.

One day, the father was going to the fair, and he asked his wife's daughters what he should bring for them.

"Fine clothes!" cried the first.

"Pearls and diamonds!" shrieked the second.

He turned to his own daughter, and asked, "My child, what will you have?"

She said, "The first twig that catches on your hat on the way home, my father." On his way back home from the fair, carrying clothes, pearls and diamonds, a sprig of hazel caught on his hat. He broke off the sprig and gave it to his daughter. She took it and planted it in her mother's grave, watering it with tears. Three times a day she wept over the sprig, and it soon became a large tree. A little bird built its nest in the tree and became her friend. He watched over her and brought her whatever she wished for.

Now, the family heard that the king was to have a feast that would last three days. At this feast, his son, the prince, was to choose a bride. Ashputtel's two sisters were breathless with excitement, because they were asked to come to the ball. They called for Ashputtel, and screeched, "Now comb our hair, and brush our shoes, and tie our sashes, for we are going to the king's feast!" She did as she was told, but she could not keep tears from sliding down her cheeks, for she wanted very much to go. She finally begged her mother to let her go.

"You? Ashputtel?" she asked in horror. "You have no fine clothes, and you cannot even dance!" When she kept begging, her mother said, "I will throw this dish of peas into the ash heap, and if you have picked all of them out in two hours, you have my permission to go to the ball."

Ashputtel ran out the back door into the garden, crying out:

> "Thrush and blackbird, hurry quick,
> Help me, help me – pick, pick, pick!"

Soon, hundreds of little birds fluttered down, stooped their heads, and started working. Pick, pick, pick, every bird helped Ashputtel to pick out the peas from the ashes. In an hour, her task was completed. She showed the dish of peas to her mother, but she scowled, and said, "No, no, no! You cannot go, you dirty little girl, for you have no clothes and you cannot dance!" After Ashputtel begged again, she said "If you can pick two dishes of peas out of the ashes in one hour, you have my permission to go to the ball." The little girl ran out to the garden, and again cried:

"Thrush and blackbird, hurry quick,
Help me, help me, pick, pick, pick!"

Her friends again came swooping down from the skies, and helped her to pick out the peas from the ashes. In half an hour, the task was done. Ashputtel showed the two dishes to her mother, but she hissed, "It is no use! You have no clothes, you cannot dance, and you would put us all to shame." And off she went to the feast with her two daughters.

Ashputtel went to the garden to sit below the hazel tree, and cried out:

"Help me, my beloved tree
Rain silver and gold all over me!"

Suddenly, her friend the bird swooped down from the tree carrying a gold and silver dress and silk slippers. She put on the lovely clothes, and followed her sisters to the ball. When she got to the ball, her sisters did not recognize her. They thought she must be a princess from a far-off land.

The king's son took her hand and started dancing with her. He was completely enchanted with her and would not dance with anyone else. They turned and twirled until late at night, and when she wanted to go home, the king's son said, "I shall bring you home," for he wanted to see where this beautiful girl lived. But she secretly slipped away from him and ran back to her house. When her mother and sisters arrived home, there lay Ashputtel in her dirty frock by the ashes. She had left her gown and shoes beneath the hazel tree so that the bird would carry them away.

The next day, the feast continued, and when her mother and sisters were gone, Ashputtel ran to the hazel tree, and said:

> "Help me, my beloved tree
> Rain silver and gold all over me!"

The bird came carrying a dress and shoes even finer than before. She hurried to the ball, and everyone whispered and wondered who the beautiful maiden could be. The king's son took her by the hand and, again, danced with her all night. This time when she went home, the king's son followed her. When she saw him following her, she jumped into a pear tree in the garden.

The king's son waited for her father to come home, and said to him, "The young lady who was dancing with me has slipped away, and I think she is in your pear tree."

The father wondered, "Could it be Ashputtel?" So he cut down the tree with an axe, but no one was in it. When he came back into the kitchen, there lay Ashputtel. She had slipped down the other side of the tree and left her fine clothes at the foot of the hazel tree.

The third day, Ashputtel again ran into the garden, and said:

> "Help me, my beloved tree
> Rain silver and gold all over me!"

Her kind friend brought her a dress even finer than the one before, and slippers made of gold. When she arrived at the feast, everyone was stunned by her beauty. The king's son again danced with her alone. When night came and she slipped away, she was in such a hurry that she left one of her golden slippers behind. He took the shoe into his hands, and thought, "This time I will not lose her."

The next day, the king's son told his father that he planned to marry the lady that fit into the golden slipper. Ashputtel's sisters were overjoyed to hear this, for they were certain they could fit their feet into the slipper. The eldest daughter and her mother went into the room where the slipper lay and tried to shove her foot inside. However, her big toe would not go into the shoe. Her mother gave her a knife, and said, "Cut it off! When you are queen you will never have to walk on foot again." So the silly girl cut her toe off and squeezed her foot into the slipper. She hobbled outside to see the king's son, and he sat her beside him on his horse, and rode off with his bride.

But on their way home, they passed by Ashputtel's hazel tree, and a little dove sitting on a branch sang:

> "Back again! Look at the shoe of thy bride!
> For she's not the true one that sits by your side."

When he looked at her foot, he saw the blood streaming down the shoe, and knew that he had been tricked. He brought the false bride back, and said, "Let the other sister try the shoe." When the younger sister tried to squeeze her foot into the shoe, it would not fit, for her heel was too large. But her mother forced the heel in so that it bled and took her to the king's son. He set her beside him on his horse and rode off with his bride.

But when they came to the hazel tree, the little dove sang:

> "Back! Look again at the shoe of thy bride!
> For she's not the true one that sits by your side."

When he looked at her foot, he saw that her white stockings had been stained red with blood. He brought her back again, and said to the father, "This is not the true bride. Have you any other daughters?" "No," the father replied, "only dirty little Ashputtel is here, and I'm sure that she cannot be the bride." However, the prince insisted that he see her.

"No, no," the mother frowned, "she is much too dirty, she would not dare to show herself."

But the prince said that he must see her. Ashputtel washed her face and hands, and curtsied before him. Then she slipped on the golden shoe, and it was as if the slipper had been made just for her. When he looked into her pale, beautiful face, he knew her, and said, "This is my bride."

The mother and sisters turned red with anger as he rode away with Ashputtel. When they came to the hazel tree, the little dove sang:

> "The slipper fits! Take home thy bride
> For she is the true one that sits by your side."

And the dove perched on her shoulder and went home with her to the king's palace.

The Magic Horns

South Africa

The Magic Horns

Once upon a time, long, long ago, there were many large and small *kraals* on the veldt in South Africa. In one of the *kraals* lived a mother and father and their little son. One day, the mother became very ill. Her skin became the color of dust, and despite everyone's efforts, she soon died. After she died, all the other women in the *kraal* continued about their work cleaning their huts and caring for their families. The children were all happy and played all day.

Only the little boy was sad. No one cared about him. His father was away all day tending his herd of cows and bulls. At night, he was too tired to cook for his son. His young son grew thinner and thinner. None of the women in the *kraal* offered to care for the boy.

So, one day the little boy went out onto the veldt and collected firewood. He carried the bundle of wood to one of the women in the village. Standing outside her hut, he asked, "Would you give me some food in exchange for the wood?"

She took his wood, added it to her cooking fire and then began to yell at him. "This is not enough wood for me to cook a meal!" Beating him, she screamed, "Go away. I am too busy feeding my own children to bother with you." Crying, the boy left.

The next day he brought two buckets of water to another woman in the village. Smiling hopefully at the woman, he said, "Look, I have brought you some water for your cooking pot. Can you give me a little food to eat?"

The woman took the two buckets of water from the boy and poured them into her cooking pot. "This is not enough water for me to make food for my family and you. Go away, and don't bother me any more." The poor little boy began to cry. Turning, he slowly walked back to his hut.

That night, after his father had gone to sleep, he crept out of the hut and went to the cattle pen. He climbed on the back of his father's bull. As the stars shown above in the clear night sky, he headed across the veldt. "I will never return to the cruel people in my father's village," he vowed. All through the night the bull walked across the veldt, taking the boy farther and farther from his father and the heartless people of his *kraal*. As dawn drew rosy streaks across the sky and the stars faded in the growing light, the boy and the bull lay down to rest.

They had hardly rested an hour or so before a large cloud of dust appeared on the horizon. It came quickly toward them. "What is that?" asked the boy, rubbing his eyes.

To his surprise, the bull answered, "It's a very large bull leading his herd of cows. He will challenge me to a fight because he will be afraid I will take his cows away from him. Don't be frightened, because I will be victorious."

The bull got up and walked away from the boy. Hugging his arms in fear, the thin little boy sat huddled on the ground, watching as a huge bull left his herd and walked up to his bull. With flared nostrils, the huge bull pawed the ground. Both bulls tossed their horns in the air and bellowed at each other, and then began to fight. The bulls fought on and on, kicking up dust, bellowing, charging, slashing, and locking horns. Finally, the huge bull turned and fled, taking his cows with him.

The thin boy ran up to his bull and wiped him as best he could. “I was so frightened you would die,” said the boy.

“I told you I would win,” said the bull. “Now, get on my back so that we can continue our journey.”

The boy mounted on the broad back of the bull, and the two continued across the hot veldt. There was little shade from the heat of the sun. The flies buzzed quietly as the wind blew softly. The boy was so tired that he fell asleep on the warm rocking back of the bull.

As the sun set, the entire veldt turned orange. Suddenly, a giant bull appeared in their path. “Get down,” said the bull. “I am very tired from my last battle. This time I will die.”

“Oh no,” cried the boy trembling with fear. “Who will protect me if you die?”

“Don’t worry. I will always protect you. When I die, cut off my horns and take them. They will give you whatever you need. Just strike them together and ask for whatever you want,” said the bull. “Now, get down off my back. I must fight this bull.”

The boy was horrified at the thought that his friend would die. Huddled on the ground, he watched as the two bulls fought on and on through the night. The struggle was fierce. Finally the boy's bull collapsed to the ground and died just as the sun was coming up.

Running to the dead bull, the boy fell on the ground and clasped his arms around his bull's neck. He wept and wept. "What will I do now?" moaned the thin little boy wiping his eyes. Finally, he rose and cut off the bull's horns, as the bull had told him to do. Leaning the mighty horns on his shoulders, he continued to walk across the veldt.

The poor little boy walked more and more slowly as the horns grew heavier and heavier on his shoulders. Just as he thought he could go no farther, he came to a hut. The man in the hut invited him to come in and rest. "I have no food, as there is a famine here. All I have is weeds to eat, but you are welcome to rest and spend the night," said the man.

The little boy remembered what the bull had said and so, striking the horns together, he proclaimed, "Please give us food and drink." Instantly, there was food and drink on the table. The man was very surprised. The boy and the man ate together. After supper, the man set a mat on the ground of the hut, and the boy went to sleep.

In the middle of the night, the man crept up to the boy and took his magic horns. In their place, he put an old pair of horns of the same size. In the morning, the boy rose and, thanking the man, took the horns and headed across the veldt.

By noon, with the hot sun high in the sky, the little boy had grown very thirsty. He sat down and struck his horns together saying, "I am hot and thirsty. Give me some water and some shade." Nothing happened. So he did it again. Still nothing happened. "How is this possible?" wondered the little boy. Then he examined the horns carefully. These were not his magic horns.

Slowly, the little boy walked back across the veldt to the man's hut. As he neared the hut, he heard the man striking the horns together and demanding food and drink. His voice grew louder and louder as he became angrier and angrier at the horns. Obviously nothing was happening. The little boy went into the hut. The man froze with fear. What power did this child have? He was not sure but he was afraid. He rushed past the boy and ran away before he could be harmed. The boy took the horns and, striking them together, demanded food and drink for himself. He ate and drank, and then went to sleep.

Then, in the morning, he once again started across the veldt with his horns. After a while he came to a large and rich *kraal*. He was hot, tired and very dusty from his journey. A woman came out and, seeing him, she began to yell. "Get out of here. We have no need for the likes of you." The little boy began to cry. He was very sad as he walked away.

"What am I going to do?" he wondered. Remembering his vow, he thought, "I will never go back to my own *kraal*, the people there are cruel." Suddenly he had an idea. He walked to a river near the *kraal*. He washed and washed himself until all the dust and dirt was gone. Touching his horns gently, he requested beautiful new clothing and brass jewelry to decorate his arms and legs. No sooner had he requested all this than it was done.

Thus, dressed as the son of a chief, he again walked to the rich *kraal*. This time the whole *kraal* welcomed him. Bowing down, the headman of the *kraal* said, "Welcome, welcome," and commanded that a feast be prepared for him. The thin little boy stayed on at the *kraal*. Everything he wanted was given to him by his magic horns. When he grew up, he married the daughter of the chief.

BAWA MERAH

South Africa

Bawa Merah

Once upon a time there lived a widow. Everyone was very kind to her. She had but one daughter, named Hompito. The widow was nice to everybody. No one knew that at home she was domineering and bossy, because when she was outside of her home, she was always humble, and seemed sweet and gentle and pious.

Even the sultan's wife was kind to her. The sultana would often ask the sultan if she could invite the widow and her daughter to join them when they went fishing. The sultan had a daughter named Bawa Merah. Bawa Merah and Hompito would play together, but Bawa Merah did not really trust or like Hompito. Something in the girl repelled Bawa Merah, but Bawa Merah was too well-behaved ever to say anything.

One day, while all of them were fishing off the rocks above the sea, the widow pushed the sultana into the ocean. There was but one cry, and the sultana was gone. The widow wept and wept, and said that she had tried to save the sultana as she fell but was unable to do so.

A year later, the sultan married the widow. At first, all was fine in the palace. The widow had so many things to do that she could not boss around Bawa Merah. As soon as the widow was settled, though, she began to mistreat Bawa Merah. To escape the widow, Bawa Merah would often ask to go fishing with the sultan. Of course, she never complained about her stepmother, the widow.

One day while they were fishing, Bawa Merah caught a beautiful, golden fish. "Please may I keep it?" she pleaded with her father.

"Why do you want it?" he asked. "What will you do with it?"

"I want to keep it as a pet in a pool in the palace," she said.

Bawa Merah brought the fish fine rice balls to eat every day. She trained the fish to come when she sang,

Il kankita
Si Bawa Merah
Si Bawa Puteri
Si Bawa Merah

And the fish would come to her.

One day, Hompito followed her to the pool and spied on her. She heard her sing and saw the fish come up and eat the rice balls. When Hompito returned to her mother, she told her what she had seen. "Do you mean to tell me that Bawa Merah is playing with a fish when she has work to do in the palace?!" said the mother, with great annoyance in her voice.

The next day, the widow took some rice balls and went to the pool and sang:

> *Il kankita*
> *Si Bawa Merah*
> *Si Bawa Puteri*
> *Si Bawa Merah*

The fish rose in the water when it heard the song. However, instead of giving the fish the rice balls, the widow grabbed the fish and threw it on the ground to die. Then she took it home and cooked it herself. She and her daughter ate the entire fish, remarking on how delicious it was. They threw the bones to the cat that had been watching everything. The cat refused to eat the bones.

That evening when Bawa Merah went to feed the fish, it would not come. For three days she went and sang, and for three days it would not come. Then she realized she would never see the fish again. That night she was very sad. She missed the fish, and even more, she missed her dear, sweet mother. As she lay crying in her bed, she heard a scratching at the door. She opened it and in came the cat. The cat jumped up on the bed and sat next to Bawa Merah.

"I was your mother's cat, and we would often talk together," said the cat, to the great surprise of Bawa Merah. "I have come to talk to you, for things have happened that you must know. The golden fish was the spirit of your dear, sweet mother. The other day, the widow caught the fish and ate it." At this, Bawa Merah began to cry even more.

"Do not cry," said the cat. "There is much to be done. The widow gave me the bones of the fish, and we must bury them where they will be safe. Come with me."

Bawa Merah followed the cat out into the garden. There, under the tree, the cat began to scratch. Soon the bones of the fish appeared. Bawa Merah gently wrapped them in clean white linen. Then she and the cat left the palace. They walked until they came to the palace of a neighboring sultan. There, in the neighboring sultan's garden, they buried the bones of the fish wrapped in linen under a beautiful flowering tree. Then they hurried home.

In the morning, the son of the neighboring sultan went for a walk in the garden. There he found a pair of small golden shoes. "I will marry the person who can fit into these beautiful little shoes," he said.

It was announced throughout all the kingdoms in the area that the son of the sultan was looking for a wife who could fit into a pair of small golden shoes. From all over, young women came, including Hompito, but none could fit into the shoes.

Then the cat said to Bawa Merah, "Those shoes grew out of the spirit of the fish bones. The fish held the spirit of your mother. Go and try them on. They will fit you." So Bawa Merah went and tried on the shoes, and of course they fit her perfectly.

She married the sultan's son, which made her father very happy because it meant that there would always be peace between the two kingdoms. Before Bawa Merah left the palace to join her new husband, she told her father about the fish and everything that her stepmother had done. The father divorced the widow and made her and her daughter leave the kingdom. From that day on, he ruled wisely.

DOMITILA

Mexico

Domitila

On a dry, dusty rancho in the state of Hidalgo in Mexico, there once lived a poor farmer, his loving wife, and their only daughter. This daughter was hard working, patient and gentle. The townsfolk said she was as sweet as a cactus bloom. Her name was Domitila.

Domitila helped her parents to build their tiny adobe casa. As she made bricks of clay and sand and laid them to bake in the sun, Mama told her stories from long ago. At the end of the stories, she would always say to Domitila, "Remember what my mother told me and her mother told her. Do every task with care and a generous dash of love."

The family had a little corn patch to supply them with food. However, they also made leather goods to trade for beans and rice, as they were very poor. One day, while the family was working on their soft leather sandals and pouches, rain exploded from the skies. Fierce waters rushed through the canyons and spread into the plains, washing away their tiny corn patch. The water lapped at their casa, and the house began to crumble. After a few hours, all that was left of the little house were two crumbling walls and a muddy floor. Domitila's mother shivered as she inhaled the musty air. Domitila tried to comfort her mother by wrapping her in shawls, but her mother coughed and gasped and became very ill.

Domitila's father looked at the rain clouds rolling in and frowned. He said, "Domitila, you could help us by going to the Governor's mansion. I hear that they are paying cooks to work in the kitchen. With what you earn, we can buy enough food to last until our corn grows again. Do not worry, I will take care of Mama."

Domitila was determined to help her family. She wrapped herself in a shawl, kissed her parents goodbye, and walked in the pelting rain to the mansion of the Governor of Hidalgo.

The chief cook at the great house put her to work right away. Domitila chopped, sliced, fried and stewed while she dreamed of returning to her poor family. One day, the chief cook said to her, "You have proven yourself to be a fine cook. Now make something good to please old Abuela and her grandson." Domitila went to work preparing her family's favorite dish.

When she served the dish to Timoteo, the oldest and most handsome son of the Governor, he asked, "What is this?"

"They are *nopales*, Señor, a food of my people," Domitila said, lowering her head in respect.

"*Nopales*? They are nothing but prickly desert weeds!" sneered the young man.

His grandmother scolded him, "We are a noble family; we must not complain about the food of common people. Show the girl respect by trying the food!"

Timoteo apologized quickly and raised a piece of the cactus to his mouth, grimacing in disgust. Once the flavor touched his tongue, he exclaimed, "Why, this is delicious! A weed has been turned into a delicacy! What is the secret?" Domitila whispered, "I have no secret, Señor. I cook the way my mother taught me," and she slipped back into the kitchen.

Timoteo did not notice that she had left because he was gobbling up all the *nopales* on his plate. "I must find out what is in this marvelous food," he said to himself.

That night, a servant awoke Domitila, saying "Your mother is very ill, so you must go home immediately."

When she arrived home, her father ran out to meet her and took her face in his hands. "Domitila," he said sadly,

"Mama has passed away."

Domitila sobbed and ran to her mother's empty bed. Suddenly, she felt a presence beside her. When she looked up, she saw her mother's spirit. It said, "I will always be with you, Domitila. Remember what my mother told me, and her mother told her. Do every task with care and a generous dash of love." As the spirit faded away, Domitila knew she would never forget her mother's words.

The next morning, Timoteo returned happily to the dining hall. He expected to be served a breakfast as delicious as his dinner of *nopales* the evening before. However, he took a mouthful of food and clutched his throat in horror. "Where is the cook from last night?" he cried.

The third cook appeared in the doorway, saying, "The second cook left last night because her mother is very sick. However, she dropped this on her way out," and the third cook placed a leather strap in Timoteo's palm. Timoteo examined the strap, which had fallen from her sandal. The leather was finely carved with flowing designs. "Could this be her work too?" he wondered.

The third cook said, "She spoke of adding something very special to anything she makes, but I do not know what she meant."

Timoteo thought about this as he rubbed his stomach and examined the leather piece. "Where does this girl live?" he asked. The third cook only knew that she lived somewhere in Hidalgo. "Saddle my horse," Timoteo called to his stableman.

Timoteo traveled toward the great plains of Hidalgo. He asked everyone he saw about the young girl who could turn desert weeds into food and leather scraps into works of art. Everyone had heard of this girl, but no one knew where she lived. He soon came upon the widow Malvina and asked if she knew this girl of many talents.

Malvina thought to herself, "So this is the rich man searching for Domitila. If I plan this right, I can get this young man for my daughter instead." She said to Timoteo, "I do know where she lives," and gave him directions that would take him far away from Domitila. "Now he will ride in circles long enough for me to carry out my plan," she thought.

As soon as he left, Malvina ran to her daughter, Pereza. Pereza was sprawled in the shade of an arbusto bush.

"Wake up, lazy girl! We're going to be rich!" she cried, and dragged the girl to a nearby pueblo. While Pereza went from house to house, begging for food at the front door, Malvina snuck around to the back and stole from the kitchens of all the townsfolk. When Malvina and Pereza got back to their hut, they cooked the stolen food. The next day, with piles of tortillas, enchiladas, tamales and chili rellenos, they walked to the rancho of Domitila's father.

When they arrived, they found that no one was home. Malvina snooped around and smirked when she saw that there was no food in the cupboards. When Domitila and her father returned, they were shocked to see food piled high on every chair and table in their house. Malvina and her daughter stood by, putting on a false show of sympathy. Domitila and her father politely ate the tasteless meal made of stolen food, as they had nothing else to eat.

Malvina's scheme worked quickly. Domitila's father missed having a wife to care for him, so he married Malvina. Malvina thought to herself, "My plan is working perfectly. It will be a simple trick to fool the young man when he makes his way here. I will send Domitila away and let him think that Pereza is the talented cook."

By the time autumn came, life was nearly unbearable for Domitila. "Make more bricks! Find more wool for Pereza's shawls!" Malvina would shout. Domitila learned what hard work was like without her mother's laughter and love. However, she endured it patiently.

Meanwhile, Timoteo continued to roam the plains for Domitila. One day, he came upon the Hidalgo Fall Fiesta. As he approached the fair, a familiar fragrance tickled his nose. He spurred his horse and galloped towards the fiesta. When he arrived, he asked an old woman, "Where is the girl who cooks *nopales* so well that I can smell them from a mile away?"

"You must mean Domitila," she said. "She makes *nopales* for the fiesta every year. Of course, we all know why her *nopales* are so delicious. She puts care and a very special love into everything she does. If you are looking for her, she is visiting her mother's grave." Timoteo thanked her graciously for helping him and galloped away.

On the road ahead, he saw a young girl walking. When he reached her, he said kindly, "Buenas dias, Señorita. I have been looking for a girl named Domitila. Do you know where I can find her?" He looked at her feet and saw that she was wearing sandals with a design that matched the carved leather strap he was carrying. As she lifted her eyes to him, a breeze gently lifted her hair from her sweet face. As their eyes met, Timoteo's heart felt like the beginning of a new day as the sun bursts from behind the Sierra peaks. "You are Domitila!" he cried.

"You must be hungry, Señor, as you have travelled a very long way," Domitila said softly. She untied her scarf and took out a tortilla filled with delicious *nopales.*

They sat by a stream, and Timoteo told her how he had searched for her throughout Hidalgo after the widow Malvina had given him directions. Domitila now understood that Malvina had created a dark plot that involved Timoteo, her father, and herself. They broke open the tortilla together, and the delicious scent encircled them. Timoteo suddenly understood the secret of the *nopales.* He thought to himself, "Desert weeds become a delicacy when they are made by Domitila. But it is her love that makes them fill my heart." They went to visit Mama's grave, as they would every year from then on. Afterward, they went to the Governor's mansion, so that Domitila could become Timoteo's beautiful bride.

Some years later, Timoteo became Governor of Hidalgo. The kindness that his wife had taught him helped him to rule gently and fairly, and he brought prosperity to the land. Malvina and Pereza fled from Hidalgo, and Domitila's father moved into the mansion to be with his daughter and her new family. Every time Timoteo saw Domitila bouncing their children on her knees, he smiled as she said, "Do every task with care and a generous dash of love, my children."

Gata Borralheira

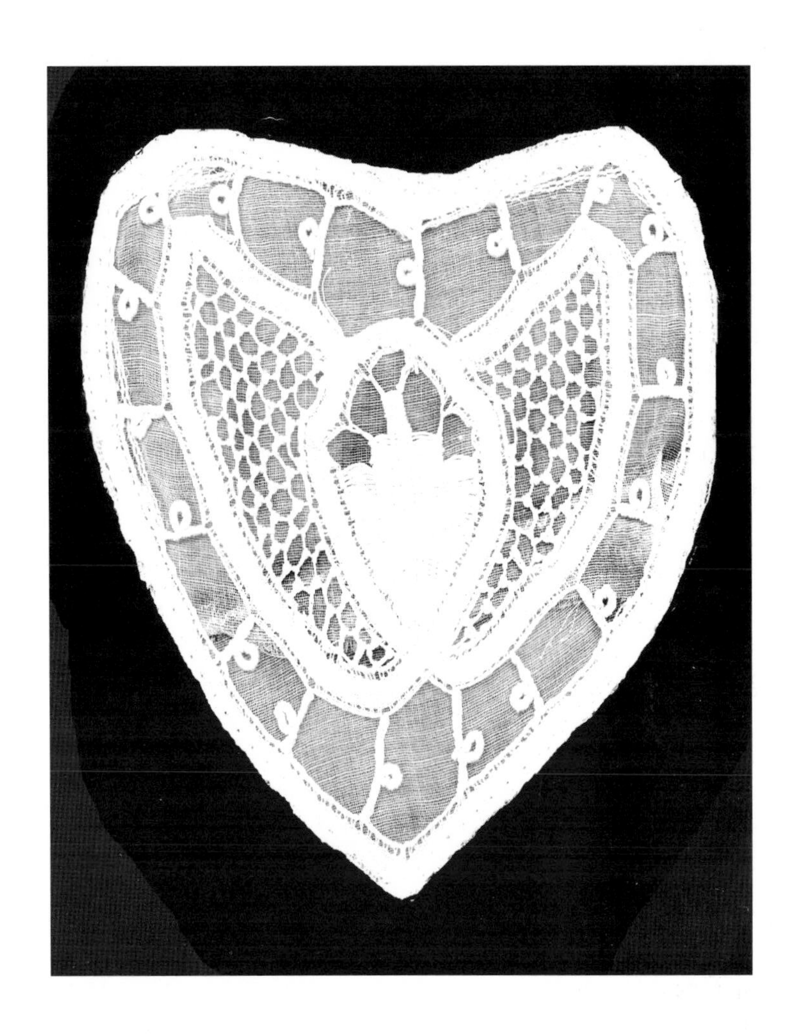

Brazil

Gata Borralheira

Once upon a time, long ago in Brazil, there lived a mean stepmother with three daughters and one stepdaughter named Gata Borralheira, which means cat's ashes. This was not a very nice name, as ashes have no value or use, and cats in Brazil can only live in the kitchen with the servants. In fact, Gata Borralheira was treated as if she were the servant of her three sisters. Her mother had been half American Indian and half African, while both of her three stepsisters' parents were Portuguese. This made them think they were very important and that she was nothing, even though they were very ugly and she was quite pretty.

Poor Gata Borralheira had no one to play with but three little mice that lived behind the stove. She loved her pet mice and took good care of them. When her sisters sent their dishes back to the kitchen, Gata Borralheira would always feed the mice before taking food for herself. Her three pet mice loved her in return.

Every day Gata Borralheira was expected to clean the house, do the laundry, and cook the meals. She was looked down upon by the family and never allowed out of the kitchen except to wash and clean up after her sisters. Everyone felt that she was just a servant. This was a terrible thing because servants in Brazil are often ignored as if they don't exist. They are not viewed as people with feelings who can be sad or have broken hearts.

Gata Borralheira missed her dead mother. She cried and cried, but, of course, since she was a servant, no one heard her or cared if she was unhappy.

One day the prince sent an invitation to every family in the city and invited them all to a ball to celebrate his birthday. Everyone was invited. The three sisters flew around the house trying on dresses, sewing on ribbons, curling their long hair, and laughing at the thought that they might get to dance with the prince. Of course, no one told Gata Borralheira to dress for the ball. After all, she was only a servant. Even though the invitation said everyone was invited, the three sisters knew that servants were not included in the invitation.

The evening arrived, and off the three sisters and their mother went. Poor, unhappy Gata Borralheira was left behind in the kitchen by the cold fire. Wiping a tear from her eye, she called her three pet mice to her. They all curled up in her lap and gently licked her fingers trying to make her feel better.

Suddenly, an old witch appeared. Gata Borralheira jumped to her feet in fear. The three mice hid in the sleeves of her worn dress. The witch just stood there laughing. It was not a cruel laugh; it was a kind and caring laugh. "My dear, dear child, don't be frightened. I am here to help you." Taking a rough stick from the fireplace she tapped Gata Borralheira lightly on the head. When Gata Borralheira looked down, she found she was dressed in a beautiful dress all a-glitter with diamonds and little seed pearls. On her feet twinkled little glass shoes.

Next, the witch gently touched Gata Borralheira's hair, and it was instantly curled and beribboned and beautiful. "Who are you?" asked Gata Borralheira.

"Why, I am your fairy godmother. I know that I look like a witch, but looks can be deceiving. Now, how am I going to get you to the ball?" Looking around the kitchen the witch spotted a large pumpkin sitting on a shelf. "Ah," she said, "this is just the right shape," and touching it with the stick she turned it into a golden coach. "Now my dear, what do you think I can use for horses?" Just then the three mice peeked out from the sleeve of Gata Borralheira's dress. "They are just the thing," said the witch pointing to the mice, and before they could disappear again, she touched them with the stick and turned them into three beautiful horses.

"Now my dear, dear girl, there is only one thing you must remember. My magic is only good until midnight. By the last strike of the clock's bells, everything will turn back into what it was before, and your beautiful dress will again turn to rags. So, be sure to leave the ball in time," cautioned the witch. Kissing Gata Borralheira gently on the cheek, she sent her off to the ball in the golden coach.

When Gata Borralheira arrived at the ball everyone was dancing and having a wonderful time. As she stepped from her golden coach, everyone stopped to turn and look at her. She was so very beautiful, her dark hair shining and her face warmed with a gentle smile. The prince was dancing with one of her three stepsisters. When the music stopped the prince bowed to her stepsister. Then he turned and walked up to Gata Borralheira. Bowing low to her, he asked her to dance. From that moment on the prince had eyes for no one else in the room. He danced and danced with Gata Borralheira, spinning her around until she could hardly breathe. He was so handsome and she was so happy.

Suddenly, the clock bells began to ring, and Gata Borralheira realized that she would have to flee, as it was midnight. She did not want the prince to see her in rags. Rushing out the door, she lost one of her slippers. She jumped into the golden coach and fled home, arriving just as the bells stopped ringing.

There she stood, back in the kitchen with the pumpkin on the shelf and her three pet mice at her feet. Had it all been a dream? No, for on her foot was one glass slipper. She took it off, and, holding it gently for fear it too would disappear, she hid it behind a brick in the fireplace. If nothing else, she would always have a wonderful memory.

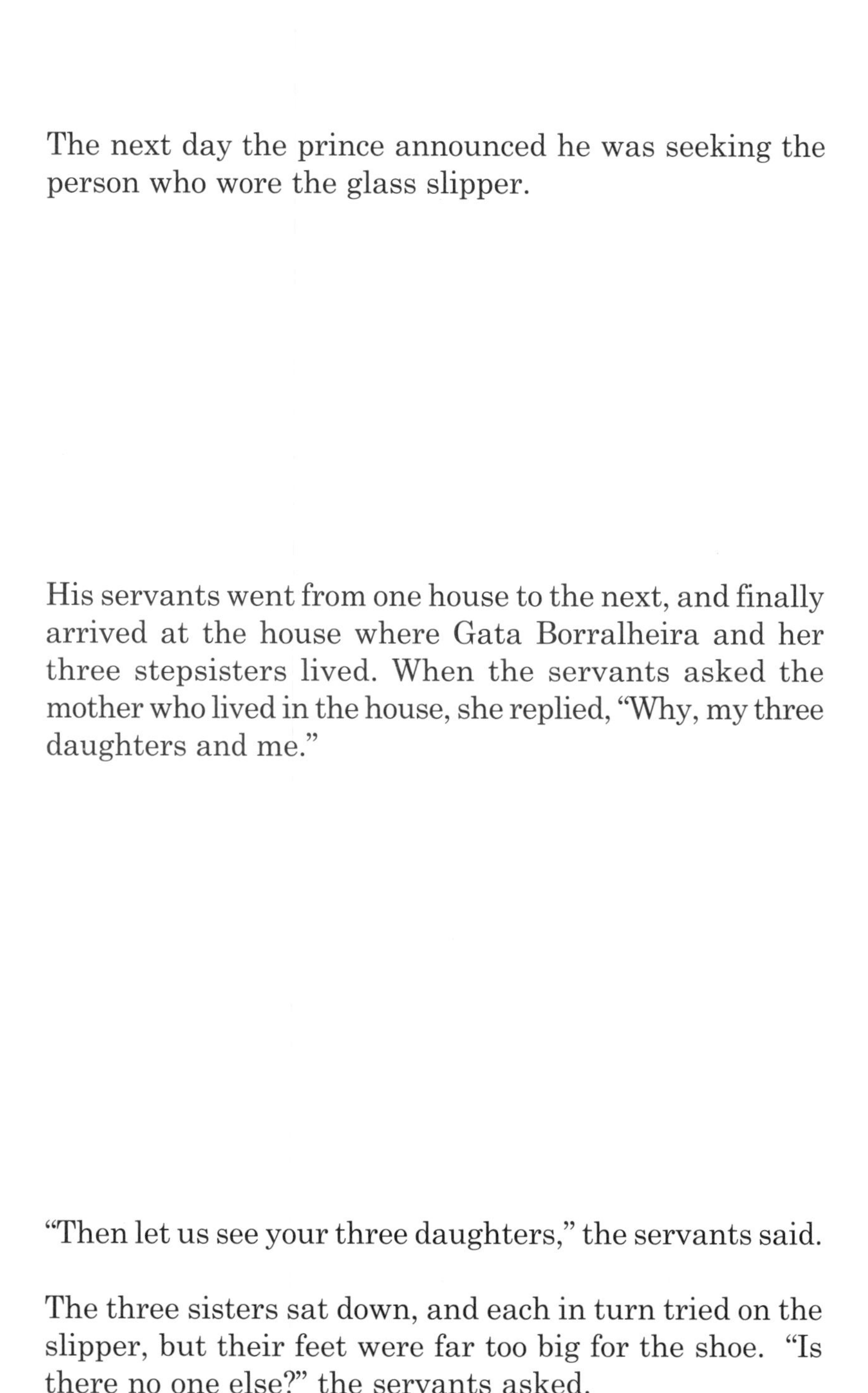

The next day the prince announced he was seeking the person who wore the glass slipper.

His servants went from one house to the next, and finally arrived at the house where Gata Borralheira and her three stepsisters lived. When the servants asked the mother who lived in the house, she replied, "Why, my three daughters and me."

"Then let us see your three daughters," the servants said.

The three sisters sat down, and each in turn tried on the slipper, but their feet were far too big for the shoe. "Is there no one else?" the servants asked.

"No, no one else," the mother answered.

As the servants were leaving the house, the three mice ran out in front of them dragging the glass slipper that Gata Borralheira had hidden behind the kitchen hearth. "What is this?" they said, picking up the slipper. Returning to the house they asked again, "Who else lives here?"

"No one," said the stepmother. With that the three mice dragged Gata Borralheira out of the kitchen.

"Who is she?" the prince's servants asked.

"She is just the kitchen servant," replied the stepmother.

"Well, even she must try on the slipper." Gata Borralheira tried on the slipper and, of course, it fit. The servants rushed to the prince, who came and got Gata Borralheira. He took her and her three pet mice away and married her. They all lived happily ever after.

The Maiden and the Fish

Brazil

THE MAIDEN AND THE FISH

There was once a widower who had three daughters. The oldest two daughters were proud, idle girls who thought only of clothing and finery. They would often sit at the window, and do nothing but daydream for hours. The youngest daughter, on the contrary, took care of the entire household. She was even fond of helping the servant in the kitchen. Her sisters snickered at this, and nicknamed her "Hearth-Cat."

One day, the widower caught a golden fish, and brought the wriggling creature home for dinner. He gave the fish to his youngest daughter to prepare, as she was the only one who cooked for the family. She liked this fish very much for his attractive golden color. She could not bring herself to cook the fish, so she placed it in a pan of water and begged her father to let it free. The father finally agreed, and she happily took it to her room. When the sisters saw her new pet, they were furious that they would be deprived of a delicious meal because their silly sister had taken the fish as a pet.

That night, as the young girl lay sleeping, the fish began to call to her: "Maiden! Please throw me down into the well!" The fish asked so kindly and desperately that she finally got up and threw the fish into the well.

The next day she peered down into the well, so that she could have a last look at her friend. She saw nothing but darkness, but heard a voice calling, "Maiden! Please come down into the well!" At first she fled in fear. But the next day, when her older sisters had gone to a festival, she again peered into the well and heard the imploring voice. She finally dove into the well, and before she reached the bottom, the fish appeared in front of her. He took her by the hand, and brought her to a golden palace. "Go into that chamber, and dress yourself in the finest robe you can find. Put on a pair of golden slippers, too, for you are going to the same festival that your sisters are attending. You will be brought there in a splendid carriage. However, as the festival is ending, you must leave before your sisters do, and bring back the dress and the shoes."

The girl slipped into a dress that sparkled with gold and precious stones, and came out of the well. Awaiting her was a beautiful state carriage. When she arrived at the palace, everyone admired the elegant girl with the rich, golden robes. They all wondered where she could possibly have come from. At the end of the festival, she was in such a hurry to get back to the well, she lost one of her slippers. The king was following close behind, for he was very intrigued by the beautiful young girl. He picked up the shoe, and declared that he would marry the maiden to whom the slipper belonged.

The girl took off her rich garments, and as she hurried out of the well, the fish told her to return in the evening, for he had something to ask of her. She hastily agreed and ran home. When her sisters came home, chatting about the golden girl they had seen at the festival, the youngest sister was busy working in the kitchen. The sisters prattled on about the king's intent to marry the mystery woman at the festival, and declared that they would go to the palace that evening to try on the slipper. If it fit one of them, she would be made queen! One of them sneered that if she were queen, she might be generous enough to give the silly Hearth-Cat a new dress.

As soon as her sisters had left for the palace, the youngest daughter went to the well as she had promised. When the fish saw her, he said, "Maiden, will you please marry me?" The maiden was horrified. "I cannot marry a fish!" she exclaimed. But the fish begged and begged, and, because the fish had been so generous, she finally consented. Suddenly, the fish was transformed into a man! He said in a gentle voice, "I am a prince who was enchanted some time ago. The king is my father, and he intends to marry the girl to whom the dainty slipper belongs. Therefore, you must go to the palace immediately to try on the shoe. When he tells you that you must marry him, you must say that you are already engaged to his son, the prince. He will send for me once he hears these words."

The maiden went home and met her sisters who were returning from the palace quite disappointed. The slipper did not fit them, and they were pouting and angry. When the youngest daughter said softly that she was thinking of going to the palace, they huffed, and said, "See what airs the silly Hearth-Cat is putting on! Aren't you ashamed of yourself? Go show your tiny feet to the king, and he will laugh in your face!" The young maiden walked to the palace anyway. When the guards saw her shabby dress, they refused to let her pass. However, the king spied her from his window and ordered them to let her in. He handed her the slipper, and it fit her delicate foot perfectly. The king was struck with wonder, and said that she was now his queen. The maiden lowered her eyes and respectfully told him that she was already engaged to be the bride of his son, who had been under a spell for so long. The king was delighted to hear that he would soon see his son, and quickly forgot his disappointment. He sent soldiers to fetch his son from the well, and married him to the beautiful young girl.

There were great feasts and festivals to celebrate this marriage, and the older sisters were enraged and bitter. They were punished for their mistreatment of their sister, and they cursed and screamed filthy words. The Hearth-Cat soon became the queen, as the prince succeeded to the throne.

Maria Cinderella

Chile

Maria Cinderella

Once upon a time, long ago, there lived an old man and his young daughter. Though it was only the two of them, they were very happy. One cold winter day, the fire in their fireplace went out. The little girl looked around for matches but could not find any. "Father," she said, "the fire has gone out. I will go across the road and ask our neighbor, the young widow, to give us a few hot coals to re-light our fire."

The day was very cold, and even though she did not have far to go, she was pinched with cold by the time she arrived at the neighbor's house. She knocked on the door. "Come in, come in," said the neighbor. She could see how cold and hungry the young girl was, and offered her some hot soup to eat before sending her home with the hot coals in an iron pot.

The next day, the young girl, named Maria Cinderella, again noticed that the fire was fading. She did not stir the coals, but instead told her father that she would go once more to the neighbor and borrow some hot coals. When she arrived at her house, the young window again gave her some delicious hot soup before sending her home with the hot coals. So the winter passed.

One day Maria Cinderella said to her father, "Father, our neighbor is very kind, and you are all alone without a wife. She says you should marry her so that I won't keep bothering her every day when the fire goes out. Why don't you marry her? She will take good care of you, and she is very kind."

"Are you sure you want me to marry again?" asked the father. "Are you sure that she will always be kind? Now she gives you sweet soup, but one day she may feed you only a cruel and bitter soup."

"Please father," Maria Cinderella pleaded, "I know she will make us very happy."

"You are very stubborn," said the father. "I will marry her but you may live to regret that you asked me to do this."

So that spring the old man and the young widow were married. She continued to be good and kind. A year passed and she had a daughter. The old man named her Maria after his first daughter. As the child grew older, she became meaner and meaner. One day she said to her parents, "Maria Cinderella does nothing but eat."

The old man looked at his younger daughter, and said, "So you are tired of your older sister already."

So he sent Maria Cinderella out into the fields to watch the cows and sheep, while her younger sister rested at home. One day while watching the cows, one began to give birth to a calf. The cow had a very hard time and died. Maria Cinderella rubbed the young calf and made *chaicancito* and boiled sheep's milk for it. She took loving care of it.

This did not please her younger sister, who was growing meaner every day. "Mother," the mean Maria said, "Maria Cinderella does nothing but play with her young calf. She does no work at all. You should give her something to do."

"What do you think we could ask her to do?" asked Maria's mother.

"Spin," replied Maria without a pause. "Give her lots and lots of wool, and tell her to spin it into yarn for weaving. Give her more wool than she could ever spin in a day, and tell her to complete it in a day."

So the stepmother went to Maria Cinderella with a full bag of washed wool. "Here," she said. "Watching the cows and sheep is not really work. While you are watching them spin this wool into yarn. If you don't spin it all, I will beat you."

Poor Maria Cinderella took the large bag of yarn and the wooden spindle whorl and walked out into the fields with the cows and sheep and her sweet young calf. She cried and cried as she walked along. Tears of pity poured down her cheeks. "Why are you crying?" asked her young calf.

After getting over her surprise at hearing the calf speak, she said, "I must spin all this wool into yarn by the end of the day or my stepmother will beat me."

"Don't cry," said the calf. "I will spin the wool into yarn for you." So they found a quiet grove of trees, and Maria Cinderella put the spindle whorl on the calf's horns. Quickly he began to spin the finest wool she had ever seen. Turning his head from side to side and kicking the spindle whorl with his hoofs he quickly spun all the wool into fine yarn. Maria Cinderella watched and rested under the shade of the trees. When the calf was done, she stood up, and the calf and the other cows and sheep which had been grazing all returned home with her. Maria Cinderella fed the young calf fine grain and fresh grass. He ate and ate, as he was very hungry after working so hard all day spinning.

Maria Cinderella gave the fine wool to her stepmother. The next day her stepmother again gave her a very large bag of wool as she left for the fields with the cows and sheep. In the evening she again returned with all the wool spun into fine yarn. This went on for many weeks. "How is it possible for Maria Cinderella to accomplish so much?" wondered Maria. "Mother, someone must be helping my sister. She could never do all this by herself," said mean Maria to her mother. "I will sneak out into the fields and watch. When I find out who is helping her, I will get even."

So the next day, Maria followed her sister into the fields and watched as the sweet calf spun all the wool into fine yarn. Maria rushed home and told her mother. "Mother, it is the calf that is weaving the yarn."

"How is that possible?" asked her mother.

"The calf puts the spindle whorl on his horns and, using his hoofs, he spins the yarn. We must get rid of the calf," she raged.

"How can you do that?" asked her mother.

"Pretend I am sick and I need the meat of a young calf. Father will kill the calf to make me better," laughed Maria.

That evening, when the old man came home he found his youngest daughter in bed weak with fever. "Dear husband," said his wife, "we must kill Maria Cinderella's calf and feed its meat to Maria so that she will get well. The old man loved his youngest daughter and was sad to see her so ill. It was only a calf, and so he took his axe and killed it. He cut up the calf and gave the meat to his wife to fix for his sick daughter. The wife took the intestines of the calf and cut them into neat even pieces and gave them to Maria Cinderella to wash in the river. "Bring me back all of the pieces of intestine or I will beat you soundly," said her stepmother.

Maria Cinderella cried and cried, but there was nothing she could have done to save her calf. Taking the intestines she went to the river. While carefully washing them an eagle came and alighted on the branch of a nearby tree. He suddenly rose up and, swooping down, grabbed one of the pieces of intestine. Maria Cinderella began to shout, but the eagle would not drop the piece of intestine. She quickly hid the other pieces under a rock so that the eagle could not get them. She began to cry even harder because she knew that her stepmother would be furious at her for having lost a piece. "Oh dear, oh dear! What can I do?" sobbed Maria Cinderella. "I am so miserable. I miss my calf, and I am afraid that my stepmother will beat me when she sees that one of the pieces of meat is gone." Overhead the eagle swooped back and forth, hoping to get more of the meat. Wiping her eyes, Maria Cinderella left the meat hidden under the rock and went in search of help.

Walking along, she came to a large house. An old lady was just coming out of the house as Maria Cinderella arrived. "Please," sobbed Maria Cinderella, "can you help me? My stepmother gave me some intestine to wash, and that eagle," pointing to the eagle flying in the distance, "has stolen a piece of it. My stepmother said she would beat me over the head if I lost any."

"Do not cry," said the old lady. "I am just off to church. While I am gone please take care of my three young daughters until I get back. Hit them if they are naughty, beat the rugs, shake out the mattresses, and clean the cinders from the fireplace. When I get back I will help you. Now wipe your eyes and don't worry."

Maria Cinderella called the three little girls to her and quickly scrubbed them clean, dressed them neatly, and sat them down on chairs where they wouldn't get into any trouble. Next she carried the rugs outside and beat them until all the dust was gone. Finally, she shook out the feather mattresses until they were soft and fluffy, and then set them on the bed frames. Just as she was done, the old lady returned from hearing mass at church.

"My, my, what a nice job you have done," said the old lady. "Here, let me give you some fresh intestines I have. Also, here is a magic wand. Whenever you need anything just take it out and wave it saying, 'By the grace that God has given you, please give me...' Only be sure to hide the wand, so that no one sees it. Now off you go. On the way home, when you hear a cock crow, lift your head up to heaven, and when you hear a burro braying, look down to the ground."

"Thank you so much for all your kindness," said Maria Cinderella, smiling. Carrying the intestines to the river she quickly washed them. Then, placing them on a tray, she covered them. Balancing the tray on her head, she started home. As she walked along she heard a burro bray. She quickly looked down. Soon she heard the cock crow. She quickly looked up. Golden stars fell on her head and adorned her forehead.

Totally unaware, Maria Cinderella quickly walked home.

When she arrived home her sister began to scream at her. "Look how dirty you are. What do you have on your head? It is disgusting. Here, take this dirty rag and cover your head before anyone sees it." Maria Cinderella's stepmother rushed in and tied the dirty rag on Maria Cinderella's head, hiding the beautiful golden star. She then sent her off to the kitchen in disgrace.

"Mother," said the nasty Maria, "Maria Cinderella looked so beautiful with that golden star. Perhaps you should say you are sick and then father can kill my calf for you. Then you can send me off to wash the intestines by the river, and I can meet the old lady, and she will give me a golden star, too."

The stepmother cackled with joy at the thought, and that very night she lay in her bed groaning and tossing with make-believe pain. Her husband killed Maria's calf and made a roast for his ailing wife. In the morning, the stepmother sent the nasty Maria to the river with the pieces of intestine just as she had done with Maria Cinderella. Even though Maria knew it was only an act, she was so frightened by her mother's threats of a beating that she cried as she left for the river to wash the intestines.

At the river, the eagle again came and stole a piece of meat. Maria quickly hid the rest of the intestines on the tray under some rocks. Then she walked off to the house of the old woman. There she met the old woman who was just leaving. Crying, Maria explained that the eagle had eaten the intestines she was cleaning for her mother, and that she was afraid if she didn't get them back from the eagle her mother would beat her. "Can you help me?" Maria whined.

"I am just going off to hear mass at the church, but when I get back I will help you. While I am gone, take care of my daughters. Beat them if they are naughty. Shake out the bed, beat the mattress and the rugs until they are clean, and burn all the junk in the house in the fireplace," instructed the old lady.

Maria called the three girls to her and beat them until they were red and bruised all over. Next she took an axe and beat the mattresses and the rugs leaving them in tatters. Finally she gathered up all the junk and broken furniture and put it in the fireplace, but she was too lazy to set it on fire.

When the old lady returned, she looked at her three daughters all red and bruised and sobbing. "I see you have done just as I asked, said the old lady. Here is some intestine I have. You may take it. On your way home you will hear a donkey bray. When you do, look up. When you hear a cock crow, quickly look down."

Maria took the intestines and went back to the river where she washed them and put them on the tray. She took a cloth to cover them, then placed the tray on her head and started to walk home. As she walked along, she heard a cock crow, and she looked down. Then she heard a donkey bray. She quickly looked up. With that, a pile of manure dropped from the sky and fell on her forehead. She dared not touch it and rushed on home.

When she arrived home, her mother saw her. She was very upset to see what had happened to her daughter. "Look in the mirror and see yourself," wailed her mother.

"Oh dear," cried Maria, "I am covered in burro dung."

"You have really made a mess of it this time," said her mother as she quickly covered her daughter's head with a fine silk scarf. All this time Maria Cinderella sat by the fireplace in the kitchen with her head covered with an old greasy rag. Under her dress she hid the magic wand. That evening, Maria Cinderella's father came to her, and said, "Didn't I warn you that first it is sweet soup and later it is bitter soup?" At last she understood what her father had meant.

The following Sunday, the nasty Maria and her mother went off to church. Maria Cinderella wanted to go too, but they did not invite her to join them. Suddenly, she remembered her magic wand. She took it out, and said, "Magic wand, by the grace that God has given you, please give me tall strong horses and a beautiful coach and clothes to wear to church." Instantly she was dressed as fine as any princess, her head covered with a beautiful lace mantilla.

Off rode Maria Cinderella to church. On arriving, she left her coach by the church door. Maria Cinderella entered the church and knelt near her stepmother and sister. Nasty Maria nudged her mother, and said, "Look, there is Maria Cinderella."

"Don't be silly," said her mother and continued to pray. As soon as the service was over, Maria Cinderella left the church and got into the coach. It rushed her home. When she arrived she took her magic wand and, using it, changed back into her old rags. When her stepmother and sister arrived, the stepmother said, "See Maria, my dear child, your sister was here all the time. That could not have been her at the church."

The next Sunday, nasty Maria and her mother went to church again. Of course, they did not invite Maria Cinderella to join them. Maria Cinderella wanted to go to church even though she had not been asked. So she took out her wand, and said, "Magic wand, by the grace that God has given you, please give me tall strong horses and a beautiful coach and clothes to wear to church." Once more, she was instantly changed. Her old ragged dress turned into a beautiful golden gown. On her head appeared a rich golden lace mantilla in place of the dirty rag. Dressed in her finery, she stepped into her coach and rode to church. When she arrived, she again sat near her stepmother and her sister.

"Look mother," whispered nasty Maria. "I'm sure that is Maria Cinderella."

"Don't be foolish," hissed her mother and continued to pray.

As soon as the mass was over, Maria Cinderella rushed to her coach and rode home. As she was leaving the church, she rushed by a prince who had also come to services. He was struck by her beauty and wondered who she was. He decided to come again the following week to learn who she was and from where she had come.

The following Sunday, nasty Maria and her mother again went to church. As soon as they were gone, Maria Cinderella took out her wand and asked again to be dressed in fine golden clothes from the tip of her head to the ends of her toes. Dressed in a shining gown with little golden slippers, she stepped into her golden coach and went to church.

When she arrived, she again sat near her stepmother and sister. Seeing her, the prince went to sit by her side. Throughout the service he stared at her, but she just bent her head and prayed. As soon as the service was over, Maria Cinderella quickly left the church. One of the prince's guards tried to stop her at the door of the church, but she rushed by losing a golden slipper in her hurry. She quickly jumped into her coach and sped home.

When she arrived home, she quickly took out her wand and changed back into her rags.

Meanwhile, the prince stood at the church looking unhappy. "How could you have missed her?" asked the prince, looking angrily at the guard.

"I'm sorry, Sire. She just slipped past, but she dropped this slipper as she ran," said the guard.

The prince took the slipper and examined it. It was truly very small. "Go throughout the kingdom and find the person to whom this slipper belongs. Try it on the foot of every young woman," commanded the prince.

The guards rushed off and, stopping at every house, they asked to see every young woman. They then tried the slipper on them. In every case the slipper was too small. "We have been to every house in the town; the young lady must have come from a rural farm. We must search further, for the prince will be very angry if we do not find the owner of this slipper," said one of the guards. The guards went to report their results. Then the prince, his favorite courtiers and his guards, who had been searching for the owner of the little golden slipper, all set off for the countryside.

Finally, the entire retinue came to the farm where the two sisters named Maria lived. The stepmother was very excited and sent for her own daughter. Seeing the little slipper, nasty Maria said, "It's mine." When she tried on the slipper it fit. Everyone was delighted. The prince sat her on the sidesaddle of the horse he had brought to bring his bride home.

As they started off, a dog rushed forward and barked,

> "Wow, wow, wow, bow, wow,
> Burro dung on horse now,
> Wrong one up there! How?
> Golden star should there sit,
> Little slipper she does fit,
> Bow, wow, bow, wow, wow."

"Get out of here," screamed the stepmother, but the dog would not move.

"Listen to what the dog is saying," said a servant. The prince got off of his horse and began to search though the house. He looked in every room and closet and cupboard, but he found nothing until he came to the oven. Inside the oven sat Maria Cinderella. "What are you doing in here?" ask the surprised prince.

"Sitting," said Maria Cinderella in a timid voice.

"I am looking for the person to whom this little golden slipper belongs," explained the prince.

"It is mine," said Maria Cinderella and placed it on her foot.

"How do I know it is yours and not that of the other Maria?" asked the prince.

"We are half sisters and have the same small feet. But only I have the matching slipper," said Maria Cinderella shyly. "Ask her for the other slipper."

Of course nasty Maria did not have the other slipper. While the prince went to ask the nasty Maria if she had the mate to the golden slipper, Maria Cinderella went out to get her other slipper. She washed and, using her magic wand, dressed herself in her golden gown. When the prince returned she showed him the other slipper. Then he went to place her on the bridal saddle instead of her sister. "I will not sit where burro dung has sat," she said. So the prince took both her and her father away on other horses. They were married in a beautiful wedding in the castle by the bishop.

Bibliography

Afanasev, Aleksandr, ed. *Russian Fairy Tales.* Translated by Norbert Guterman. New York: Pantheon Books, 1973.

Bushnaq, Inea, ed. and trans. *Arab Folktales.* New York: Pantheon Books, 1986.

Coburn, Jewell Reinhart, ed. *Domitila: A Cinderella Tale from the Mexican Tradition.* Auburn, CA: Shen's Books, 2000.

Dundes, Alan. *Cinderella: A Folklore Casebook.* New York: Garland Publishing, Inc., 1982.

DuPlessis, I.D., ed. *Tales from the Malay Quarter.* Translated by Bernard and Elize D. Lewis. Cape Town: Maskew Miller, 1945.

"Gata Borralheira" told by Liza Papi.

Grimm, Jacob, and Wilhelm Grimm. *Grimm's Fairy Tales.* New York: Puffin Books, 1994.

Hayes, Barbara. *Folk Tales and Fables of the World.* Illustrated by Robert Ingpen. New York; Portland House, 1987.

Louie, Ai-Ling. *Yeh-Shen: A Cinderella Story from China.* New York: Puffin Books, 1982.

"Maria Cinderella" told by Elizabeth Van Ulstein.

Pedroso, Consiglieri, ed. *Portuguese Folk Tales.* Translated by Henriqueta Monteiro. New York: Benjamin Blom, Inc., 1969.

"Red Onion, White Onion" collected in Bali.

Seki, Keigo, ed. *Folktales of Japan.* Translated by Robert J. Adams. Chicago: University of Chicago Press, 1963.

Tatar, Maria, ed. *The Classic Fairytales.* New York: W.W. Norton and Company, Inc., 1999.

Illustrations

Akar, Azade. *Authentic Turkish Designs.* New York: Dover Publications, Inc., 1992.

Appelbaum, Stanley, ed. *Traditional Chinese Designs.* New York: Dover Publications, Inc., 1987.

D'Addetta, Joseph. *Traditional Japanese Design Motifs.* New York: Dover Publications, Inc., 1984.

Linenthal, Peter. *Russian Folk Motifs.* Mineola, New York: Dover Publications, Inc., 1998.

All other illustrations were taken from the personal collections of Ila Lane Gross and Willard Vine.

Cover illustrations, clockwise from upper left: China, South Africa, Russia, Japan, Brazil, Chile, Indonesia, Saudi Arabia.

Back cover illustrations, clockwise from upper left: Mexico, Germany, India, Turkey.